Luke 17:2

(A Memoir of Abuse, Recovery, and Triumph)

Michael Emerton
and
Patrick Emerton

Copyright © 2013, 2016 by Stone Cellar Publishing. Portsmouth, NH

Notice

Mention of specific individuals, companies, organizations, or authorities in this book does not imply endorsement by the publisher, nor does mention of specific individuals, companies, organizations, or authorities in the book imply that they endorse the book. All other information has been attributed to the appropriate source.

All rights reserved. No part of this publication may be reproduced or transmitted in any form or by any means, electronic or mechanical, including photocopying, recording, or another information storage and retrieval system, without the written permission of the publisher.

Edited by: Jennifer Netzer Hartley, Neil Turitz, Victoria Piercey

Book cover designed by: Tracy Dow, Mosaic Communications: www.mosaiccommunications.com

For additional content, please

Visit us on the Web: LUKE172.com

Follow us on Twitter: Luke172@luke_172

Find us on Facebook: Luke172

Email us: Luke@luke172.com

ISBN 978-0-615-73194-0

Contents

Chapter 1:	THE WHIRLWIND IN DALLAS	1
Chapter 2:	FEBRUARY 2002	2
Chapter 3:	THE SPOTLIGHT TEAM	4
Chapter 4:	CANADA	9
Chapter 5:	CAMPING	16
Chapter 6:	LOOK HOW FAR YOU'VE COME	23
Chapter 7:	THE INMATES ARE IN CHARGE	26
Chapter 8:	THE FIRST DREAM	28
Chapter 9:	PEW	29
Chapter 10:	IT JUST GOT PERSONAL	31
Chapter 11:	TWO JOBS	33
Chapter 12:	CALLING ME BACK	35
Chapter 13:	VEGAS	37
Chapter 14:	WHO AM I?	44
Chapter 15:	MISSION	47
Chapter 16:	RESPONSE	50
Chapter 17:	GAME FACE	52
Chapter 18:	GOT A PLANE TO CATCH	54
Chapter 19:	THE CONFERENCE	58
Chapter 20:	WE THE PEOPLE	64
Chapter 21:	IN THE CHAMBERS	68
Chapter 22:	TO THE CENTER	70
Chapter 23:	THE CONVENTION	75
Chapter 24:	FEET TO THE FIRE	81

Chapter 25:	DISSENSION	88
Chapter 26:	BANNED	92
Chapter 27:	NEW JOB NEW OFFICE	98
Chapter 28:	THE GOVERNOR	102
Chapter 29:	AT THE GATES	104
Chapter 30:	THE SECOND DREAM	108
Chapter 31:	THE WORLD TURNS	109
Chapter 32:	THE CARDINAL	114
Chapter 33:	THE PHIL DONAHUE SHOW	118
Chapter 34:	BREAKING THE RING	120
Chapter 35:	LAW MUST GO!	123
Chapter 36:	THE OPERA HOUSE	127

CODA	129
ABOUT THE AUTHORS	130

Luke 17:2

It were better for him that a millstone were hanged about his neck, and he cast into the sea, than that he should harm one of these little ones.

PREFACE

This memoir tells the disturbing, but true story of how I dealt with my demons created by the Roman Catholic Church. In telling my story, I hope that others will gain insight as to why it's so difficult to come forward. I know that every abuse experience is different, every emotion is unique to the individual, and every journey to recovery is an individual's own effort to find peace of mind.

To place a statute of limitations, an expiration date, on the prosecution of sexual abuse is absurd. Shame, pride, social standing, and the perceived impressions of friends, mothers, sons, daughters and wives all eat at a victim's conscience. And there always seems to be the headlines—Penn State and Jerry Sandusky, Boy Scout sexual abuse cases, and additional revelations regarding Catholic Church improprieties—to agitate long hidden emotions. Reactions to normal, daily events become exaggerated. I've found myself punching walls sometimes because my nine-year-old is playing at a friend's house, and I didn't know the family well. I've sat, shaking uncontrollably, after dropping my son off at daycare because I can't get the image out of my mind that he is being molested there.

For those struggling to come forward, questions assail... How will I be viewed? What will people say behind my back? Am I now the brunt of pedophile jokes? "Hey, you are the guy who…"

Well, for me, this book completes a journey begun ten years ago when my dammed up memories burst free upon reading the *Boston Globe's* coverage of the Catholic Church sexual abuse scandal. That's when I found out that I was not alone. I then reluctantly did a job that needed to be done and prayed for my release upon its completion. Now, I have come full circle and hope that these pages will help others realize the intricate emotional struggles of victims and praise those who come forward to expose injustice.

I want to take this opportunity to extend a heartfelt apology to the Voice of the Faithful members and to the journalists to whom I could not find the courage to reveal my past. I also want to reiterate my love for my wife, Janis, who stood by me through this madness. Please understand that when your soul is on fire, it is impossible to explain your actions and emotions. You just want the pain to stop and to return to a sense of normality.

And these days, I'm still struggling to comprehend what is normal.

~ Michael Emerton

Ever since the *Boston Globe* reminded the world in 2002 about the power of journalism, about the role the 4th Fourth Estate has in keeping our governing institutes in check by asking the questions that keep transparency in place and dialog flowing—ever since the *Boston Globe's* Spotlight Team exposed the Roman Catholic Church's sexual abuse scandal, I have been trying to write the story of what happened. I have been trying to tell the tale of all those I know who have been abused.

I grew up in a parish in which dozens of my friends were abused and raped—and one killed—by a priest who had molested and raped boys in his previous parish. I wrote for ten years knowing that I was missing the point, knowing that no matter how rich the emotions, the textures of the places, or tones in the words, I couldn't write the story because it wasn't my story to tell in the same way that it was my brother's. So, for ten years I continued to fill out my concentric rings of plot while leaving the middle blank… until the summer of 2012, when my brother handed me his seven-hundred-page manuscript and asked if I could find a narrative in it.

The result is a book of voices. It is my voice in my brother's voice. It is his voice in the voice of many. It is voices in e-mails, at podiums, and from the democratic process. It is the probing voice of the press, the child's in the adult's, and hopefully a voice that will make us all take heed before we repeat the mistakes of history.

****

I dedicate this book to the Honorable Constance M. Sweeney for her judiciousness, BishopAccountability.org (Terry McKiernan, Anne Barrett Doyle) for its importance, and The Globe Spotlight Team (Martin Baron, Ben Bradlee Jr., Matt Carroll, Kevin Cullen, Thomas Farragher, Stephen Kurkjian, Mark Morrow, Michael Paulson, Sacha Pfeiffer, Michael Rezendes, Walter V. Robinson) for being journalists in a time when they are hard to find. Thanks are due to Mike Dempsey, James MacGillivray, Jason DePerrio, and Thomas McCarthy for their friendship and guidance; my mother for her mysticism; Theresa and Chris (for being my bro and sis); and my dearest Kelly for her warmth, sweetness, and shine. A special thanks to the Survivor's Network of those Abused by Priests [SNAP], to Barbara Blaine, and all those who refuse to keep silent no longer.

~ Patrick Emerton

Luke 17:2

(A Memoir of Abuse, Recovery, and Triumph)

In 2002, lawyers sifting through Catholic Church files discovered a secret document that outlined a template of procedures for clergy to follow for instances pertaining to the discovery of priests sexually abusing the laity. The document was so sensitive that it was ordered stored in the archives of each diocese, never to be published or commented upon—with excommunication from the Catholic Church for anyone violating this directive.

The 39-page document, titled in Latin Crimen Sollicitationis, was issued in March 1962 by the Holy Office. The document outlined procedures for the crimen pessimum, or "worst crime," —homosexual acts contrary to a priest's celibate commitment—and imposed an oath of secrecy on the victim, the priest dealing with the allegation, and any witnesses.

These secret procedures were discovered in the footnote of a May 18, 2002, letter from Cardinal Joseph Ratzinger to the Catholic Church's bishops regarding new procedures for sex abuse cases. (Ratzinger was head of the Vatican's doctrinal congregation before becoming Pope Benedict XVI in 2005.)

Crimen Sollicitationis was enforced for 20 years by Cardinal Joseph Ratzinger before he became the pope.

1. The Whirlwind in Dallas

At first, it was windy and white in there, and then it was clear, and then it was nothing but dizziness and fear. All I could hear was the buzzing of my nouns and ideas whirling around. A tornado had formed. It had taken all the buildings, lifted the cars, and snatched all the Lone Stars. All the media trucks, satellite dishes, sidewalks, bishops, journalists, chalices, pews, crucifixes, and Jesus statues in existence were pulverized into windy white dust bits that flew around my face. Then I was the only one there. There was just a question and me. The gust, which had given birth to the question, had blown everything away, leaving me and the question:

"Are you a victim?"

I watched her lips form it. I saw each word walk off her lipstick and into the microphone.

"Are ... you ... a ... victim?

Before she could ask it, all I could hear was the sound of feet tapping, tapping, never-ending heels and toes clacking, clopping, stomping, getting louder by the day until that reporter asked this question that blew everything away:

"Are you a victim?"

2. FEBRUARY 2002

All eyes were on the TV. The New England Patriots were in the Super Bowl, and the whole family was cheering. Everything was great, except for that newspaper. My mother brought a copy of the *Boston Sunday Globe* to the party, and on the front page there was an article titled, "Priest Says He, Too, Molested Boys." In the story was the name, "The Rev. Ronald Paquin," and it revealed that Paquin's name had appeared in documents related to another priest, the Rev. John J. Geoghan, who was being tried for the sexual assault of a minor. The article stated that Paquin, too, had left a trail of victims over a 25-year period in Methuen and Haverhill, Massachusetts. A black-and-white picture of him was included with the article.

He was a middle-aged man, medium build, slightly overweight with a potbelly, brown hair, and large round glasses. My mother showed me the article before the game. Sitting in the corner of the room, I glanced at the picture and blinked. Time seemed to freeze. All the excitement of the pre-game faded away; all the people in the room were gone, and I was sitting there alone staring at a picture of Paquin.

"You spent a lot of time with Father Paquin," my mother said. "Did he ever try anything with you?"

Her words came to me as if echoing down a large sewer pipe. I was lost for a moment in the silence. I wasn't feeling anything. I wasn't breathing. I wasn't thinking. I just felt thick and numb, like there were packing peanuts all around me, and then I felt my emotions rush down that pipe.

"No," is all I said, with the same passion as if someone had asked me if I wanted salt.

"Really?" my mother replied. "You went camping with him, and that trip to Canada, and he never tried anything?

My reply, again, simply, was, "No."

And that was that. I passed the newspaper on so that someone else could comment, but I didn't hear the comments.

I turned back to the Patriots. The whole experience was creepy. I never felt that kind of numb before, and it scared me. At that moment, I could have walked past a car crash with my family injured inside, surveyed the scene, then kept walking to go get an ice cream. No sadness. No happiness. It was almost as if I didn't exist at all.

But soon I was back and waiting for the Patriots to win that game, the excitement was enough to remove the name, "Paquin" from my mind, if only for a little while.

3. THE SPOTLIGHT TEAM

In 2001, The *Boston Globe* began chronicling the sexual abuse trial of a priest named John Geoghan. By the end of February 2002, it was clear that Cardinal Law and his predecessor both knew of the abuse, yet approved Geoghan for transfer, time and time again, which resulted in him abusing children wherever he went. Hundreds of them!

By the end of February, the frequency of the stories had picked up. On a daily basis, new headlines were thrown on doorsteps and popped up on computer and TV screens. Everyone was talking about them, and it was becoming clear that this Geoghan incident was not isolated. Each headline seemed to reveal deeper secrets as the Globe's Spotlight Team unearthed more and more bones from the Catholic crypt: "Officials Avoided Confronting Priests over Abuse"; "Church Settled Six Lawsuits Against Priest"; "Scores of Priests Involved in Sexual Abuse Cases"; "Woman Says Church Ignored Her Outcries"; "Church Cloaked in Culture of Silence."

The Archdiocese of Boston was the fourth largest in the United States, spiritual home to more than 1.8 million Catholics. My hometown, Haverhill, Massachusetts, was 75 percent Catholic. Every time I read, or heard, one of these stories, that creepy numbness set in. It lasted longer each time. But I had nothing to say, other than, "What scumbags!" or "It's unbelievable!" Each headline got me angrier, and as I got angrier that festering numbness transformed into something else. I still can't define it, and I didn't know what it was back then, but it was always there, eating at me, weighing me down, and pulling me closer to its frozen center.

I didn't want to hear these stories! But I couldn't miss a word. One morning on my drive to work it seemed as if every station was talking about the Catholic sexual abuse scandal. *Don't think about it! It's not your problem! It's not your mess! You have gone too far in your life to let any of this get in your way.* But I couldn't turn off the radio. I was transfixed. A sharp pain ran up my neck.

Tears filled my eyes. The road became blurry. I looked at myself in the rear view mirror, all red-eyed, flustered, and angry. *You can't go to work looking like this! What the hell is the matter with you? You've got a ton of crap to do today, and you want to walk in looking like someone just died? What would you tell your colleagues?*

I had to clear my head, move past this, and get on with my morning. If I could do that, everything would be okay. At the Trailways bus stop off Route 95, Exit 3 in New Hampshire, there was a quiet place at the far end of the overflow lot. It was a good place to put on my game face. I sat there watching the trees blow, trying to pinpoint exactly why all this was bothering me so much. After all—*it's not my problem, right?* "Right!" I said to myself. But I was wrong. It was indeed mine, and it was a very big problem.

Day after day, for weeks, I frantically spun the dial trying to get away from those stories, but sooner or later I always gave in and listened. Then the tears and the pain in my neck came, forcing me to pull into that bus station. Parked up back by myself, my thoughts would travel to my childhood... to where I grew up alongside the Merrimack River.

My father was a Vietnam vet who survived the physical war, but lost the mental one. He turned to alcohol. Oftentimes he would sit in a chair in a dark room for days. I would walk by the room and think there was a shadow or a ghost there—I never dared to enter. He was mostly absent from my childhood and he died in 2001 of cancer in his early 60s. Just days before he died, my mother told me that he said, "I wish I could have done more to change the church." That statement still haunts me to this very day. I still wonder, *What the hell did he mean by that?*

My mother was the rock of our family, and her stability came from the Roman Catholic Church, but her power seemed to have a source below its surface. Beyond the pages of the Bible and under the pews there was a mysterious pool from which she drew a deeper understanding of God and spiritual matters. Being a Carmelite nun for six years (before marrying my father, and having my oldest brother, Pat) immersed her in mysticism. Then, due to my father's absences, she turned to that one place she could trust. In our case, that was St John the Baptist Church in Haverhill's Riverside neighborhood.

To earn extra money, she began cleaning and cooking in the rectory. While she did this, my sister, two brothers and I, ran around the parking lot and rolled down the grassy hills flanking it.

The priests were always friendly. At times, my mother would have them over for dinner—an event I would brag about the next day in school. For the first fourteen years of my life, the church was fun. And as I grew, so did my faith. I went through Sunday school, First Communion, and I became an altar boy. However, my mother being a former Carmelite meant she was one of Saint

Theresa's followers, one who understood *The Dark Night* and lived *The Ascent of Carmel*, one who could examine inwardly in ways that *normal* Catholics couldn't. The legend went that the Virgin Mary promised that all those who died clothed in the garments of Carmel would be saved.

Well, this seemed good to me. All I had to do was wear a string around my neck with two pieces of brown cloth representing the garments of Carmel tied to it. It was called a "scapular." If I wore it morning, noon, and night, and recited the Rosary I was assured that the fires of Hell wouldn't touch me. So, I put on the scapular! *Nothing will ever harm me.* And every night, I said the rosary while looking at the Stations of Cross in a book. This helped me focus on the suffering of Jesus—and after a while euphoria set in, creating a happy, peaceful feeling. Not a bad way to fall asleep.

My nightly reflections were leading me to deeper church connections. So much so, that my mother was sure I would enter the priesthood. And for a while, I thought that would be a good path.

I was an altar boy, as were my brothers and many of our friends. I enjoyed it. I liked hanging out in the sacristy before Mass and talking with the priests. I became part of our parish's Catholic Youth Organization (CYO). One of my favorite memories is going to Disney World when I was thirteen with the CYO. Father B. tried to chaperone about twenty of us kids. Fun for us! But I think it pushed him over the edge. Shortly after that he asked for a transfer, and then a new priest named Ronald Paquin came.

This guy seemed different from most priests. He was young, in his 30s, short, with a potbelly. He arrived at Saint John's (the shortened name of Saint John the Baptist's that we preferred) from Methuen, Massachusetts, and came with really cool toys. Father Paquin drove a white, '79 fully loaded, '79 Toyota Celica Supra, which stood out compared to the other priests' cars. He also rode a Honda motorcycle, which he kept parked by the back door of the rectory. I naturally gravitated toward this new priest with the toys.

After being there for no more than a week, he invited me and a few other boys into the rectory, and up to his room. His bedroom was at the top of the stairs to the left; there was a sitting room to the right. In the sitting room, he had a small dorm-room refrigerator. He welcomed us, and told us to have a seat, and then went to the refrigerator, and offered us beer. My eyes lit-up! *No way! We can really have a beer? Now, this is a priest I can hang with!*

He was so cool, kind, and close to God. Visiting the church after school, hanging out and having a few beers, became my routine, although, the offering of beer didn't come every time. Sometimes, we just played cards in the living room. I didn't question why he wasn't offering me a beer. I knew there was a chance that he could get in trouble for it… that's why everyone kept silent about it.

Soon, Paquin was taking me for rides on his motorcycle. The first time I jumped on, I grabbed the rear seat bar with my hands behind my back. But he reached back, took my hands off and put them around his waist, and said, "If you want to ride with me, this is how you do it."

One time, he let me drive his motorcycle around the church. I was just a skinny kid and, failing to make the turn, I had to lay the bike over on its side. Thank God it had luggage compartments that prevented the motorcycle from laying flush on the ground or I would have banged up my leg badly.

Anytime he offered to take that Supra out, I was all for it. I just thought that car was the best. As time went on, and he got more comfortable with me, he would ask me questions as we drove. One day, as we cruised through downtown Haverhill, he asked, "Have you ever measured the size of your penis in a toilet paper roll?"

"What?" I replied.

"Yeah, that's the best way to judge the length and thickness of your penis."

At the time, I just chalked that up to him kidding around. My friends and I would always say those types of things to each other, so it didn't seem too unusual.

"Do you like breasts?" Father Paquin asked as he finished a beer one day in the sitting room.

I had to think about that. I thought he might be testing me in some sort of priest-way. He had a direct connection to God, after all, and I had to watch what I said.

"You mean, like, woman's breasts?" I asked.

"Yes, woman's breasts. I don't understand the fascination with them. They're just big mounds of flesh."

"Yeah, I guess so," I stammered back.

After these types of conversations, I found solace in the thought that he was a holy man, and that he must have some reason for everything. *I don't understand Jesus as he does, nor have I been trained in the seminary, so who am*

I to question anything that this guy does? There's a good reason, and I don't want him putting in a bad word to God about me.

My visits with Paquin became more frequent. After school, when I let my mother know that I was going to see him, there was a sense of relief and pride on her face.

Sometimes, before he said Mass, I would visit him in the sacristy. "I'm going to sit in the front row, stare at you and make faces until you laugh," I told him one day.

"That's fine," Paquin replied.

"OK, you'll be sorry," was my retort.

I walked out of the sacristy, around the corner, and to the pews. There was plenty of room in the first row, right in front of the pulpit. I sat down. He came out. He had eyes that looked slightly larger than normal due to his glasses. The corners of his mouth were slightly turned down, and he often seemed to be in the process of a sigh. My challenge was to make him crack-up. I couldn't use my fingers to stretch the corners of my mouth, or my hands to squish my cheeks. I had to be subtle. I had to stare him down with bulging eyes and employ spastic eyebrow movements. That way, if he did crack, then I could quickly look as surprised and bewildered as the rest of the people at Mass.

When sermon time came, I was ready. Paquin approached the wooden pulpit, adjusted the microphone, inhaled deeply, and began to sermonize. That's when I locked onto his eyes while bugging out mine. Nothing! I quickly changed to the single bulging left eye, then just the right and then a quick switch to the left again. It was all in vain; Paquin's face remained stoic and unchanged.

4. CANADA

In the summer of 1981, I was standing in the rectory after Mass. Father Paquin approached me with a question: "Do you want to go with me on a trip to Yarmouth, Canada?"

"Yarmouth? What the hell is in Yarmouth? Sounds boring," I replied.

"No, it will be fun. We can take my car, and I'll let you drive in Canada," he said.

"But I don't even have my learner's permit yet."

"Don't worry. Nobody will arrest us, or even give us a ticket. I'm a priest. Who's going to arrest a priest?"

Sounded good to me! Diplomatic immunity while traveling through Canada—*we can get away with anything.*

Then Father Paquin did something I thought was strange. After the other altar boys had left, and it was just Paquin and me, he grabbed the bag of money that had been collected at Mass and began counting out bills.

"What are you doing?" I asked.

"A little spending money while we're in Canada," he replied.

"So, you can just take money if you want to?"

"Sure, it's all money that goes to the church. I'm part of the church. We need this for gas and food in Canada," he said to me without batting an eye.

His rationale seemed to make sense. It's all money that goes to the church for such services as the CYO and Father Paquin's part of the church; therefore, it's all being spent appropriately. *Right?*

Father Paquin drove the Supra up Interstate 95, from Haverhill to Portland, Maine. The plan was to load his car onto a boat, and then shuttle to Canada. Once there, we would drive to a home owned by one of his friends, where we would stay for the first night. Then, we would drive around some more and explore a bit the next day before ending up in a hotel the final night.

The boat ride turned out to be a ten-hour gambling cruise. The ship was named MS Caribe. Six decks shuttled people from Maine to Canada, from June to September. Two decks for guest rooms and vehicles and another full of gift shops, boutiques, liquor stores, another with restaurants, a pool, and a casino. The final floor had a cinema, and chairs for catching rays.

I was so excited! I had never been on a large ship like this, nor had I ever been out of the country. I wanted to explore every corner. My eyes widened as we moved along the decks; my voice squeaked with excitement. After exploring the shops and eating in a restaurant, we ended up in the casino. It was an amazing place! All the lights, all the sounds, and the people running around—I had never seen anything like it. I also knew that I was too young to gamble. There was a sign stating so: Minors are not allowed in the Casino.

"We can't go in there. I'm too young," I said to Father Paquin.

"Don't worry about it; you're with me; nothing will happen to us."

"Well, okay," I thought. We entered the casino.

"First things first," Father Paquin said, "I notice that your Coke cup is empty. Time for a refill! You wait here."

He went off to the bar and ordered two beers. He took one of the beers and poured it right into my empty Coke cup. "Now that's more like it. This will get things going," he said. We then began walking around the casino, checking-out the tables and slot machines. I had forty dollars of my own, and I turned twenty of it into quarters for the slot machines. I was doing pretty well, too, up at times and down some others, but overall doing pretty well. I must've been there for more than an hour, and I started to feel pretty buzzed from the beers. An announcement notified gamblers that the casino would soon be closing. I had a few quarters left, so I put them into a slot machine and pulled the handle.

Two of the three wheels spun wildly. One was sluggish, it stopped on BAR. As the other two began to slow, I saw the fruit shapes and the BAR symbols pass. The anticipation reminded me of watching contestants on the Price Is Right as they spun the wheel trying to win a spot in The Showcase Showdown. The fast wheels slowed, and then sure enough two BAR symbols came-up next to the first one!

Lights flashed on top of the machine, and change began to pour out. "Holy Shit, I won!" I said, as quarters filled the tray and spilled onto the floor.

I was wearing a dark brown, leather cowboy hat I'd bought on the CYO trip to Florida. So I removed it from my head and began dumping in handfuls of quarters.

"This is amazing!" I said, gazing deep into the pile of quarters sitting in my hat. "How much do you think is here? Five hundred? Seven hundred?"

"I don't know, but we need to cash it in quickly because the casino is closing," Father Paquin said, as he nervously looked around. The slot machine's flashing lights and loud sounds began to attract attention. A tipsy fifteen-year-old winning the jackpot did not look good.

"What do you mean cash in?" was my retort. "This is cash!"

"Yes, but you don't want to be walking around with pockets full of quarters, we can turn this into Canadian money," Father Paquin said as he grabbed my hat.

We went to the cashier. Paquin handed my hat through the window. The total winnings amounted to about eighty US dollars. It seemed like a million. The cashier handed Paquin my winnings in Canadian dollars.

"What's this? Play money?" I turned to Father Paquin and gave him a whimsical look.

"These are Canadian dollars. They're just as good as US Dollars, and you can spend them on anything while you're in Canada," he said.

"Oh, you're so smart," I replied.

Father Paquin seemed to feel that we had drawn enough attention to ourselves. I was a minor, and I shouldn't have been in there, much less be drinking beer. The whole event left him a little drained, so he suggested that, in order to rest, we go to a cabin that he had reserved. I was all fired-up. The last thing I wanted to do was rest! He, however, was insistent. We went to the room.

The room was small and painted completely gray. An uncomfortable toilet was on the left side, and bunk beds ran along the right-hand wall. Between the two walls, on the back wall, was a small sitting area with a chair and a foldout table. Father Paquin lied down on the bottom bunk and motioned for me to join him.

"What? I don't want to lie down and take a nap!" I protested. "We need to go out and explore this ship some more. We need to find a casino that's open."

"No. I'm tired. We just need to get a few moments of rest," Father Paquin replied as he patted the mattress in front of him.

"No way," I said. I leaped onto the ladder that was used to climb to the top bunk. It wasn't secured, and it detached from the bed. I began hopping up and down on it like a pogo stick.

"Stop that and just lay down!" Father Paquin said. His voice sounded annoyed. I thought I'd better appease him, and lie down for a while. *After all, he is paying for the trip.* I approached the beds and began to climb to the top bunk.

"No! Down here with me," Father Paquin patted the bed again in front of his chest, this time with more force.

"Why do I have to go down there with you? There is a perfectly good bunk up here on the top," I said.

"I want you to lay down with me," Father Paquin said with an exasperated, deep sigh.

I looked into his face, and he seemed hurt by me not wanting to lie with him. I began to feel guilty. He's taking me on this trip and paying for it all. I then reluctantly lied down, close to the edge of the bed in front of him. Father Paquin took his arm, wrapped it around my waist, and pulled me close. My entire backside was pressed up against his front. It was a tight grip, and there was no getting away from it.

I lied there with my eyes open, staring at the toilet that was now right in front of me. I felt uncomfortable but yet obligated to do it. *He is a caring man of God so, naturally, he may act differently than normal folks.* I laid there for what seemed to be hours then until the beer took its toll, and I drifted off.

When I woke up, I immediately jumped out of the bed and said, "Okay that's enough sleep! It's time to go back up on the decks." Father Paquin looked at me with sleepy eyes but agreed to accompany me to the decks.

Eventually, we arrived in Yarmouth. We had to wait in his Supra for what seemed to be like forever for our turn to drive out. Eventually, our turn came and with Paquin at the wheel, we proceeded onto Canadian soil.

After driving for a while, we stopped to grab a bite at a small roadside pub. "When do I get my turn to drive?" I asked him.

"You can take the wheel right after lunch," he said.

"Yeah, baby!" was my reply. I wolfed down my food and was ready to go. I put my cowboy hat on and climbed behind the wheel. In my mind, I was Burt Reynolds from "Smokey and the Bandit," and it was thrilling to drive the Supra through the twisting roads that lead to his friend's house. I sang, "Eastbound and Down," as I cruised through Canada. *This is the greatest thing ever! It just doesn't get any better than this.*

We arrived at his friend's house, which was large and rather creepy. His friend had some kind of problem. He was either in the hospital or dead.

When we entered the house, it smelled like a nursing home and, judging by the furniture, the pictures on the wall, and the knick-knacks, this person had to be at least ninety. As I glanced around, I felt like I was trespassing in someone's memories.

I found my way to the bathroom so that I could pee. It smelled old and dingy, like the other rooms. I looked around and then opened the medicine cabinet. It contained more prescription bottles, eyedroppers, and tubes of medicine than I had ever seen.

"Holy shit," I cried, "this guy probably died right here in the house!"

A chill ran up and down my spine. I did not want to be there. Father Paquin tried to reassure me that it was okay by telling me that nothing would happen and that we were perfectly safe. But the falling night made the house turn black, and my stomach sank.

We went up to the bedroom to watch TV. Again, Father Paquin told me to sleep in the bed with him. Even though I found this weird, I didn't seem to mind it as much as I did the on the boat trip because this time I was a little scared and wanted someone close by. Paquin held me to him. I shut my eyes. *I just want morning to come, so I can get the hell out of here!* Then I said a Hail Mary, and an Our Father for insurance, closed my eyes tightly, and I fell asleep.

The next morning, bright and early, we were on the road and out of that creepy house. I wanted to put as many miles between the house and me as humanly possible. The next day was fairly uneventful. We switched off driving, some more "Eastbound and Down," did some sightseeing, and made a stop at a liquor store.

"Getting some beer?" I asked.

"No," Father Paquin replied. "Something a little bit better to go with the Cokes you like." *Sounds good.* He went into the liquor store and bought a large bottle of Bacardi. Looking at the bottle, I scrunched my nose and asked, "What's that taste like?"

Paquin looked at me and said, "It's good, and will give your Coke a little extra kick."

We eventually ended up at a motel for the night. I was far more comfortable there. It was a standard room, nothing fancy, with a bathroom, color TV, and twin beds. To pass the time, we decided to play Sorry. Father Paquin unwrapped the glasses that came with the room, plopped some ice cubes in them, and then liberally filled each glass with rum, topping them off with a splash of Coke.

"Try this, see how you like it," Paquin said as he handed me a glass.

The first taste was really strong, and I registered my displeasure with a look of consternation.

"Well, we can just add a little bit more Coke to it then," Father Paquin responded, as he poured some of my drink down the bathroom sink and added more Coke.

"Better?" he asked.

I still thought it was strong, but I did not want to be a baby, so I replied, "Yeah, that's all right.

We began playing the board game. The rum and Coke tasted better with every glass he handed me, and he was drinking right alongside me. Eventually, the rum got to me, and everything began to spin. With great difficulty, I tried to get up and go to the bathroom, falling several times along the way.

"That's enough for you," Father Paquin said. "It's bedtime."

I was lying on the floor. I couldn't see straight. The whole room was spinning. Father Paquin picked me up, undressed me, and laid me in bed. And then, just like it did in that creepy old house, it all went black. The next thing I remember was waking up in the morning. The room stunk like rum. Everything stunk! And it sickened me.

I got out of bed and ran to the bathroom to drink a glass of water. The room was spinning. I noticed I was in my underwear, and I began to wonder if anything had happened. I gulped down my glass of water. Father Paquin was standing beside the bed when I returned, he too in his underwear. His potbelly hung over the waistband. He put his glasses on.

"How are you feeling this morning?" he inquired.

"I feel like shit," was my only reply.

"Do you remember anything from last night, Mike?" Paquin asked.

"I remember playing the game, and then trying to go to the bathroom. That's about it," I told him.

A big smirk came across his face, as he adjusted his glasses. It gave me that same creepy feeling I had in the old person's house the night before. Shivers went up and down my spine. Again, I found solace in the notion that this man was a representative of God, a person that would never do me harm. *It's not him; it's you! It's a sin to think he could do anything to you.* I tried to put those thoughts out of my mind, but then all of a sudden it was like there was two of me in there, in my mind. Another side of me began talking: *What are you doing sleeping in a bed with a grown man? There's something weird about that, and he is always trying to cuddle!* Then I heard myself tell myself, *Oh, for Christ's sake! He's a holy man and full of love. That's why he expresses it in a different way than others do. There's obviously a good reason for what he does. Who are you to be questioning a priest?*

5. CAMPING

That summer, Paquin took me and a number of boys from St. John the Baptist on an overnight camping trip in New Hampshire, claiming it was part of his duties as head of the CYO. There were five of us: me, my older brother Pat, and three of his friends. Pat was among the most popular kids in the sophomore class of Haverhill High School, as were his friends, and I was looking forward to this trip as a means to climb the social ladder. *If I can get in with this group, I will have it made. Everyone will know my name; I will walk into any party and be able to talk to the prettiest girls.*

Pat had his driver's license, so he and his friends followed Paquin and me as we drove the Supra toward the White Mountains. I wanted to ride with my brother and his friends, but Paquin insisted that I travel in his car. He pouted when I brought up the idea. "I'd rather you ride with me," he said, speaking mostly through sighs.

"We are going to the same place," I said, "I'll meet you there."

Rolling his eyes, he replied, "I have no one to ride with."

"Fine," I said. I got in and left it at that.

On the way to the camp, we made a stop at a packy, where Father Paquin bought several cases of beer. We all knew that he would buy us beer—that was the reason to go. Father Paquin would rationalize his actions by saying, "Well, you boys are going to find alcohol and drink, anyway. At least this way, you're safe with me." These statements made perfect sense to fourteen, fifteen, and sixteen-year-olds. After all, everyone on this camping trip had been to keg parties on top of abandoned ski tows, on the far side of the pond, and down long, dark dirt roads that wound past the old Jewish Cemetery on the border of New Hampshire—those were the perfect places to drink. Almost every weekend someone would get a keg, or two, ready to go, and for a few dollars you could get a red plastic cup, and squeeze your way to the tap. The events were wildly popular, and the police rarely broke them up. Nonetheless, a chance to get some beer without having to fight for it was a good reason to go camping with a priest.

Upon arrival, the first things unpacked were the cases of beer. We all grabbed one and began to set up the tents. I gravitated to my brother and his friends to help them, but I noticed Father Paquin looked pouty again as he unpacked his tent. Guilt got the better of me, and I went over to help him.

The campsite was large enough for three or four tents, and it had a good-sized stream running next to it. After camp was set, we all went down to the stream with the coolers, plopped our butts in the water, and began to pound beers as the river flowed around us.

"Hey! Beer me!" was shouted as an arm extended straight up from the stream. Whoever was closest to the cooler would dig in and toss over a cold one. As more beer was consumed, aims got worse, and cans started to bounce off the rocks on their way to the outstretched hands. Spewing beer was a party foul, worthy of ridicule. The only way to redeem yourself was to grab the can quickly before it sailed downstream, place your mouth over the hole, tilt your head back and pop the tab.

"Shot gun it!" Everyone would chant.

I caught most of the cans thrown to me, and the ones I missed fell without being punctured. However, every now and then when I threw up my arm and said, "Beer me!" I would hear, "Get it yourself!" from one of my brother's friends. I guess they didn't want to take orders from the youngest. Clearly, I had some work to do if I wanted to establish myself with this crew.

I paced my drinking. I didn't want to become the stumbling drunk, slipping on rocks, or throwing up in the stream. A scene like that would get around the school quickly and be difficult to live down.

As night fell, we got out of the water and sat around the fire. Hot dogs and s'mores were on the menu. The rolls sopped up the beer in my stomach, and I began to sober up, but not much. Soon, the conversation turned to girls, and to insulting the other campers. I waited my turn to interject something funny, and then I sat back to see how it was received. I wanted to say something memorable without sounding stupid or slurring my words. The conversation went well into the evening. When it was time for me to retire, I was proud. I made it without passing out, like a couple of the older guys did. I had planned to sleep in Pat's tent with his friends, but Paquin had other ideas. He insisted I sleep in his.

I told him, "No way! I want to sleep in my brother's tent." The last thing I wanted was to be seen as the only one sleeping in Father Paquin's tent. I knew it was coming, though, the pouting, the sighs, and the guilt as Paquin pressed his point. "I just want you to sleep in my tent," he said, rolling his eyes to the top of his skull. "I have no one to sleep with."

"I want to be in their tent," I said motioning toward to my brother's tent. "They're having fun."

Father Paquin looked at me and said, "I'm not fun?

Someone must have overheard our conversation from inside my brother's tent and said, "Sleep in Paquin's tent, there is no room in here!" I guess nobody wanted the youngest in his tent, so I turned back to Father Paquin and replied, "Fine!" Then I crawled slowly into his tent.

Inside, his sleeping bag was zipped wide open. I flopped on top of it wearing shorts and a T-shirt. Paquin began to pull at my shirt and shorts and told me it was more comfortable to sleep in just my underwear. I put up a rebuttal, but Paquin insisted, and pulled my shirt over my head. The beer was catching up with me, and the tent began to spin. I wanted to throw up. And then I stopped resisting. I let him take my shirt off and remove my shorts. I turned on my side to face away from him. He crept up next to me, and pulled me in with his arm around my waist, and then it all went black, again.

In the morning, I woke up lying on my back without any covers. The sun was shining on the tent, and it began to get hot and uncomfortable. Father Paquin woke up, looked at me, and began to run his fingers up and down my bare chest.

"Does that feel good?" he asked.

"It kind of tickles," I replied.

He started up by my neck, and then he slowly moved down to the waistline of my underpants, each time moving past the band a little farther. It felt a little relaxing, kind of like when my dad rubbed my back while trying to wake me up before school, but just the fact that Paquin was doing it made me uncomfortable. *Am I supposed to be uncomfortable?*

By the third or fourth pass, his hand had moved on top of my groin and encircled my penis. He stopped there and scratched at some yellow stains on my underwear, saying, "This could be sperm. It always dries yellow and ends up smelling like bleach." He took his index finger and put it under his nose, sniffed, and then said, "Yup!"

Then he began whispering over and over in a robotic fashion, "Nothing sexual will happen between us. Nothing sexual will happen between us. Nothing sexual…" After confirming the bleach smell, he returned his hand to my waistband and began to move his fingers beneath the surface. I sat straight up against the tent wall and stared at him. Without saying a word,

I grabbed my shorts and T-shirt, franticly unzipped the tent, and went into the fire pit area.

Shaking, I looked around the campsite. Everyone was still in his tent sleeping off the night of drinking. I walked around the pit a couple times, and then I had to get away from the campsite. I started following a trail along the stream. I went for a long walk. *What the hell just happened? Father Paquin just stuck his hands down my pants! Why me? Is there something about me that says, "I'm gay?"*

I needed to get my head together and stop shaking. Far away from the campsite, I splashed some water on my face. Just before I placed my cupped hands into the water, I looked at my reflection. *I'm not gay. I like girls!* Then I dipped my hands deep into the water and began splashing it on my face.

I sat there by the stream, in silence, for a long time, just staring at the water rushing past the rocks. It was right there and then that I vowed I'd never tell anybody what had just happened. It was just too embarrassing. If it ever got around school, I wouldn't live it down. It was hard enough being a freshman without that hanging over my head. Peer pressure was brutal. If you had a zit on your nose, you got shit for a week, got caught walking down the hallway with your fly down, and the ribbing could last a month. However, being known as the boy who got felt up by a priest on a camping trip, I would never recover from that! No one would want to hang out with me, and I would never get a date. No, I would have to bury this deep inside and never speak of it again.

I slowly made my way back to the camp and noticed that most of the guys were now up, and wandering around. A sickening feeling began to settle in the pit of my stomach as I surveyed the crowd. *Did anyone hear what Father Paquin was saying to me in the tent? Does anyone know?* I began to shake again as I moved deeper into the campsite.

"Where have you been?" one of the boys asked me.

"I woke up early and went for a walk," I replied. There weren't any additional questions. I don't think he really cared. I looked around the camp for Father Paquin and found him sitting on a large flat rock down by the stream. He was wearing white shorts with blue stripes, a blue shirt with white stripes, and blue Nike sneakers. He must've been washing something; he had a bottle of dishwashing liquid and some forks and knives by his side. My brother Pat snapped his picture. Paquin had a look of surprise like he just got caught with his hand in the cookie jar. I turned away and tried to find something to do.

After that camping trip, I didn't see Father Paquin after school anymore. No more visits to the rectory, no rides on his motorcycle, and no drives in the Supra. I didn't talk to him any longer either and avoided him wherever and whenever I could. It seemed that I had escaped by never talking or thinking about that camping incident again. It was just a weird thing that happened. I dealt with it, and that was the end, or so I thought.

Summer then turned into fall and the fall into winter. I had nothing to do with Paquin and managed to keep my distance. However, without missing a beat, Paquin moved on to a new group of kids, younger kids, and yet it never dawned on me that he was running his hands all over them. I just assumed that I was the only one, an isolated case… until the morning of November 28, and I walked into the kitchen. My parents were in a state of shock.

"What's the matter?" I asked.

"Jimmy died," my mother replied.

Jimmy was Pat's best friend and a very close family friend. He was always hanging around our house and going on summer vacations with us. My mother was very fond of him. Jimmy was tall and slender with blonde hair, a kind boy with a great sense of humor, and very good at sports. I ran on the cross-country team with him at Haverhill High. He always finished at the top, and I always finished near the bottom.

The upperclassmen loved to pick on the lower-classmen. Atomic wedgies, or having your head dunked in the toilet, were standard. But if an upperclassman started to come my way, Jimmy always stood-up for me by fending off the attack.

I could not get my head around what my mother was telling me, "Dead? How? Why? What do you mean he died? How did it happen?" I fired questions in rapid succession.

Paquin had taken Jimmy and four of my brother Chris's friends, all of whom who were all about 13, on another one of his trips to the White Mountains. This time they stayed in a private chalet in Bethlehem, New Hampshire. Years later it was revealed that Paquin, as usual, kept the boys up all night long, drinking. On this trip, Jimmy was the victim as Paquin climbed into his sleeping bag. The next day, Paquin fell asleep at the wheel while traveling down Interstate 93 south in Tilton, New Hampshire. According to one of the other boys in the car, Jimmy tried to grab the wheel when he fell asleep, but it was to no avail.

The Lincoln veered off the road, rolled down a hill, and threw Jimmy out. The car then rolled on top of him.

One of the boys in the accident told me that Jimmy didn't die right away. Upon hearing this, I had that sickening, creepy, feeling in my stomach again. Although I wasn't on this outing, I knew exactly what had happened. Memories of my trip with Paquin to Canada a few months earlier, when I woke in my underwear with a massive hangover, came back—memories of us both stinking like rum—and I wondered if he was okay to drive then, but I remembered being too hung-over to tell, and that I fell asleep as he drove back to the ship. I guessed I was one of the lucky ones.

I could say nothing to comfort my mother when she told me, I just walked away to be by myself and cry. *Who is this guy? How can a man of God bring so much pain? What did we do wrong to deserve him? What is the reason God is doing this?* I was outraged and ashamed for keeping his pedophilia a secret. *Could I have prevented Jimmy's death by telling someone about the camping trip? Would anyone have believed me?* I was hyperventilating and felt like passing out. So many different thoughts went through my mind. I couldn't process them all.

Devastated, the whole city went to Jimmy's wake. A line, several hours long, twisted for blocks. Paquin said the funeral Mass at St. John the Baptist. A simple yellow booklet was handed out with Jimmy's high school photo on the front. In large bold, copy across the top it read, "JIM BOY." It was an affectionate name that only Paquin called him.

I sat with my family during the funeral. Cries and wails burst from the pews and echoed off of the altar where I had once served. I hated this church now! To me, it was a festering pile of misery. If I could have, I would have burned it down and wiped it off the face of the earth.

I looked up and saw Paquin with his hands raised above Jimmy's coffin, and listened to him say, "A darkness has come upon us, O Lord, and out of the shadow we offer our prayers." "The Human Touch" was then sung, and the Mass was over. The blasphemy of Paquin saying Jimmy's funeral Mass was inescapable to me. I determined right then and there that I was moving away from the church. I attended Mass less and less and then, finally, stopped going. There was nothing for me there. I looked up to the sky. *I see how you ruin things you prick! And I don't want any part of it!*

More than 20 years later sitting in that overflow parking lot and listening to the abuse stories on the radio, I was brought back to all those terrible memories. The stories brought me clarity. I was not an isolated case of sexual abuse by a Catholic priest. I was one of the hundreds, maybe thousands of children who had been abused.

But still I continued to put it out of my mind. God, you and I had it out a long time ago! I don't want any part of your church and what you do there. It's your problem, not mine!

I pushed it away and took comfort in my work accomplishments. I knew how to do my job and did it well. I was following my plan: *Get into shape, marry a beautiful young woman, get a high-paying job, purchase a house in an affluent community by the sea, and be well respected.* I had carefully built my narrative castle with thick accomplishment bricks. Any time one of those Catholic sexual abuse stories started knocking on my walls, I'd pour molten lead all over it. But one day, it was as if I was being assaulted by endless waves of Huns.

My stronghold started to crack and, inside, I could see a scared little boy. *No! I'm strong! I will not let this interfere with my life!* And so it went, back and forth.

6. LOOK HOW FAR YOU'VE COME

Things were going well in March of 2002. The high-tech company I was working for had just announced a new software product. It was my job to make sure that the news was covered in all the proper publications. Our company had recently announced that there would be a spin-off company. Being the Senior Director of Global Public Relations meant that I had a significant amount of stock coming my way. This was going to be my windfall, my post dot-com payout. As the date for the public offering approached, it seemed as if nothing could stop me.

Then the *Wall Street Journal* published an article saying that our company was the subject of a Securities and Exchange Commission investigation. It was disclosed that there were accounting issues in the Asia Pacific unit. The spin-off was being delayed.

A battle for survival began. We hired a law firm and an accounting firm to conduct a review. The Associated Press picked up the investigative story. It was now my job to create new stories to show that our spin-off, despite all this, had positive momentum. Meetings were being constantly held. I placed stories in all the major New England papers saying that the new start-up was relocating its global headquarters to Portsmouth, New Hampshire, and would be providing work for 300 new employees—positive spin.

It was a small victory, but a victory nonetheless; but the whole time I was crafting and placing news stories regarding software, the front page headlines continued to bring new accusations regarding the Catholic Church's sexual abuse crisis. I couldn't hide from it. It penetrated every moment of my day. I tried to block it out. This is not your problem, and they're getting what they deserve. But reading *Boston Globe* headlines such as, "DA Gives Names of 49 More Priests" made me wretch, and yet I read on… "The Boston Archdiocese late Thursday turned over to authorities the names of 49 priests it says have been accused of sexual abuse of children, bringing the number of priests whom the church has named to as many as 87, in referrals to prosecutors in the past eight days. This is the first time that the archdiocese has notified authorities of allegations of sexual abuse by priests. In the past, the allegations had been handled privately, if the charges were found to be legitimate, the victim received a cash settlement from the church and the offending priest was sent for counseling or placed on sick leave."

Due to stories such as that, the Boston Archdiocese retreated into a bunker, fortifying their walls with silence, ordering that no public announcements be made as to why they had not released that information earlier. But, the *Globe's* spotlight was right on their position, and it soon became clear that the hierarchy had known for decades that they had pedophile priests in the ranks. The *Boston Globe* was proving that they chose to protect the reputation of their shepherds, over the safety of their flock.

The stories revealed how the church had sent armies of lawyers into the homes of its victims to hand out hush money and impose gag orders. Policemen, teachers, government officials and parents who knew that sexual crimes were being committed and agreed to be silent about it, became unknowing participants in the scandal's continuation. They agreed to the money and the silence because each was told that their case was an isolated event. No one knew that their child's abuse was one in a long series of abuses, one of thousands, one of hundreds of thousands, perhaps one of millions once all the possible names are collected from all the possible files kept in every chancery from Boston to Beijing. No one knew there were other children because every time it happened, the secret was kept.

But for the people in the pews, who were used to being silent, submissive, and unquestioning, an awakening was happening. They began to look into the integrity of their leaders and to make a distinction between the religion and the church. *Are they telling us one thing from the pulpit and conducting the opposite behind our backs? Is the church actually harboring criminals? Is there such a thing as a bad priest? When we put money in the collection basket, how much is going to settle sexual abuse cases? Is the reputation of the church more important than the safety of the community? How widespread is this problem?* The people in the pews saw a difference between their church and their faith. There was dissension in the pews.

Then one man in the pews named James Muller, a cardiologist and Nobel Peace Prize winner, had a notion after Mass one Sunday. It occurred to him that there might be other Catholics who shared his concerns. Mr. Muller waited in the vestibule after Mass to talk to Father P., the priest at St. John's in Newton-Wellesley, Massachusetts. His request was simple. Mr. Muller wanted a place where he could discuss the crisis with other concerned Catholics. Father P. refused at first, but then agreed to, "Think it over and consult with others."

After a couple of days, Father P. called Mr. Muller and offered him a place on Monday night in the church basement. After the 11 AM Mass the next

Sunday, Father P. looked up and noticed that the congregation was still sitting in the pews, no one was leaving. He asked Mr. Muller if he would take the microphone.

"Um, Hello, My name is James Muller. Father P. and I, we thought that it might be useful to share our reactions to the revelations that are occurring." He looked out across the pews. There was tension and silence. Then the lone tear tear-filled voice of a shaking woman broke the silence, when she said, "I don't know what to tell my children.

7. THE INMATES ARE IN CHARGE

In March, Sacha Pfeiffer of the Globe's Spotlight Team ran a story titled, "Treatment Center of Priest Called Site of Abuse." The story covered how Father Paquin was sent to Our Lady's Hall in Milton, Massachusetts, and it went on to reveal that the Archdiocese had been using Milton Hall to house sexually abusive priests. It illustrated that there was a serious lack of oversight in that place. In an interview with a young man whom Father Paquin had repeatedly molested in Haverhill, the man told stories of the abuse he suffered at the hands of Paquin, even in Milton Hall. *These guys dropped the ball all over the place! Even when they knew the individual was a sexual predator, they still let them have overnight visitors. It's absurd!*

It made me wonder about a mindset that would allow this to happen. Was it that the sexual offender was being overseen by God? — That God would heal them and ensure their proper behavior? Was it that they believed the Holy Spirit would guide the immoral predator onto firmer moral ground? Was it that the institute was corrupt and hypocritical? Were the priests wolves in sheep's clothing? Well, whatever it was, or whatever combination of things caused it, one thing was certain: even the treatment facilities were places where, under the guise of 'supervised care,' a priest could rape a child who came for a visit.

Midway through that story, it was mentioned that the young man was introduced to Paquin in 1988 when he was an altar boy at St. John the Baptist in Haverhill. The young man was quoted as saying, "He immediately wanted to start being my friend." He said that Paquin often took him shopping, bought him gifts, and invited him to visit the church, where they would talk about religion. The story illustrated how grateful the boy's father and stepmother were that a priest had taken an interest in their son.

I walked from the kitchen into the bathroom with the morning papers and a cup of coffee. I knew I couldn't read them if people were around because they were beginning to hit me too hard. The look on my face would show that something was wrong. So, I began seeking spots where it would not look out of place if I disappeared for fifteen minutes, or so—the best place for that was the bathroom.

I began spending a lot of time in the bathroom. So much time that I worried that my wife Janis would soon ask me to get my bowels checked. I kept returning to Sacha Pfeiffer's story, and the way it chronicled the young man's relationship with Paquin. After about seven months, the man revealed that Paquin began to invite him on day trips to shopping outlets in Maine, and, eventually, on overnight trips to a camp in Kennebunkport. Before long, their conversations during the ride up Route 95 took a sexual turn. The man said that Paquin would steer the conversation toward psychology, then Freud, then sex. "He just started making this a part of our normal conversation," the young man said. "It was embarrassing at first, but Paquin would say, 'I know this is weird and embarrassing, but it's normal to talk about sex, and it's good to feel comfortable with your sexuality,' and then I'd listen to what he'd say." During one visit to the camp, the man said that Paquin began talking about massage therapy, and then he began massaging his back and legs. "Next thing you know he's fondling me," the man said. *There it is! The exact same Father Paquin that I know! —"I'm a man of God, so it's okay to bring up sex while I fondle you."*

Memories of Paquin asking me if I had ever measured my penis with a toilet paper roll, and memories of him asking me about women's breasts rushed into my head, sending blood to my face, pounding my temples, and shaking my body into a cold sweat. I wondered why this was affecting me like this. It was so long ago, done and over with! I had moved on…way on! And then there was that familiar voice, *"You're not going to let this affect you, are you? You're tough, strong and in command of every aspect of your life! Aren't you?"*

I felt sorry for the individual in the story and guilty that I didn't tell someone about Father Paquin, but who would have believed me? No one would have listened to me. Priests were irreproachable. Any attempt to discredit the good name of a priest placed the accuser's family into public shame. It seemed the church knew this, and it caused its victims to fold, to be silenced. But there was no way in hell I wanted this crap creeping back into my life. I just figured that it would pass, and in six months, everyone would move on to the next thing, and all this Catholic sexual abuse nonsense would be forgotten. So, I continued to go into bathrooms to recompose, and I continued to wake-up in the middle of the night full of sweat, gazing at the ceiling, with my heart thumping in my chest.

8. THE FIRST DREAM

It's very dark. I can't see a thing. A profound sadness is in my soul. I can't stop crying. There are many hands reaching out of the darkness to comfort me. I can feel them caressing me in an attempt to calm me down. No words are spoken, but the hands are silently communicating that "It will be all right." The darkness is gone. I find myself walking down a long dirt road. I'm now dressed in a simple white robe, as I stroll through a desert. There is someone coming my way. I stop to ask her where I am, where I'm going. The person points to a large grass hut in the distance and says, "Go there and listen." I enter the hut to find a large group of people, dressed like me. They are sitting in a circle on a dirt floor listening to a gentleman in the center speak. I take a seat in the back and turn to the center.

I'm now walking away from the hut, down that same dirt road. There is a sensation that I have been visiting the hut for some time now. There's a person walking toward me, dressed in the same type of garment. He stops to ask, "Where am I?" I recognized him right away; he's an old high school acquaintance. "I don't know where you are, but you should go over to that hut and listen to what they have to say." I then point to the hut in the distance and walk past him.

The scene changes and I am now the one speaking from the center of the circle to the white-robed attendees. I am trying to convey something, to explain what it's all about, and give them direction, but I can't quite get my point across. I have the extreme urge to help them somehow. Then it hits me! "My God, why didn't I think of this before? Why, it's so easy, all you have to do is…" But I can't finish the sentence. I've been silenced. I struggle to spit out the remaining words, but I can't. I grow weaker and very tired. Slowly, I sink to the dirt floor and lie down. A crowd approaches me as I try harder and harder to spit out the words. The more effort I give to convey my sentence, the brighter I become. I am emitting an enormous amount of light now, and people are turning their heads in an attempt to protect their eyes. I hear my words echoing in my head, "No! Wait! Wait! It's so easy… It's so easy! All you have to do is…" The entire hut becomes a brilliant ball of white light, and then everything is gone… As my eyes slowly focus on a black square.

It's the fireplace in my bedroom. I blink half a dozen times to make sure I am awake. The rest of the room comes into focus. Turning my head, I look at the clock. It's 3:00 AM, and I know that's all the sleep I'll be getting.

9. PEW

It was unusually warm one weekend in March. As a distraction to the news, I decided to refinish an old church pew. It was a present from my brother, Pat. It had suffered through a flood in the basement. The small pew had rot on the seat, cracks in the back, and its legs were beginning to pull away. I dragged it out of the basement and to the end of my driveway. I applied varnish remover and watched the bubbles ooze. They rose up out of the goo and folded in upon themselves. I stared in silence.

"Why are you trying to save that?" asked a neighbor who was walking his dog past my driveway.

"I know it's a little rough, but it has some character," I replied.

The guy looked at the ooze, wrinkled his nose, and said, "That's an awful mess!" He gave the leash a tug and continued on his way; I returned to my task.

After about four or five layers of the sticky mess, I had to drop the scraper and wipe my sweat. "This is nasty!" It smelled bad. The more I scraped, the darker the ooze underneath became, and the more strands there were dripping off the scrapper. The more layers I removed, the more sticky stringy strands there were winding around my arms, and burning my hands. "You can't get away from this stuff!" I said. "It's all over the place!" I wiped off the scraper and my hands. Looking at the mess in the driveway, I said, "I'm going to need more rags, a bigger trash bag, and gloves."

After hours of scraping, and a trash bag full of rags, the beauty of the bench emerged. I got down to the original wood and was impressed with what I saw. There were well-defined lines of grain scrolled across the seat. Some were straight, some made a ripple effect, and others seemed to swirl. Underneath the ooze, each line was playing its own role in the seat's symmetry. Admiring it, I heard a voice from another gentleman, "It's a beautiful day for a project." Grabbing one of the few clean rags I had left, I wiped my hands and looked up. "It certainly is, my friend," I replied.

"Looks like you're redoing some sort of old bench," the gentleman said.

"Yep. An old church pew I got from my brother."

Surveying the backside of the bench, the gentleman said, "It seems a little rough."

"Yeah, but look at it from this angle," I said. "Check out the texture on that seat."

He came around and looked. "Wow, that's some nice wood!" he replied. "Bet it took you a while to get down to that."

"It did," I said.

The gentleman looked at the bench again and said, "It seems like a lot of work, but I think you're right, when you're done, you'll have a nice bench. Well, good luck, and have a nice day." And off he went.

I spent the rest of that afternoon working on that bench, knowing that it was not going to be done soon, knowing that it was going to take a considerable time to refinish but also knowing that, in the end, I was gonna have a really nice church pew!

10. IT JUST GOT PERSONAL

In April, the stories became even more personal. The *Globe* ran one titled, "Suit Ties Boy's Death to Abuse By Priest." This stuck to me like the ooze from the bench. Years before Jimmy was killed, someone had complained to the pastor of St. Monica's Church in Methuen, Massachusetts, that Father Paquin had molested him and other boys from the parish. The part of the story that really got me was that this man gave his report less than a year before Jimmy's death. The man said that the pastor in Methuen, the Rev. Roche, told him that he had "taken care of the matter." *Methuen is the next town over!* Blood rushed to my face, my temples pounded. I wondered how many times these things could have been avoided.

The story went on to say that "in November of 1981, Jimmy Francis was 16, returning in the pre-dawn hours from a New Hampshire outing with Paquin and three other boys, when their car rolled over on Interstate 93, ostensibly because the road was icy. Jimmy Francis was pinned beneath the car and died of asphyxiation." But according to the Spotlight Team's inquiry, a wrongful death lawsuit was now being filed because "the road was not icy at all, Paquin had been drinking heavily and fell asleep at the wheel, and just a few hours earlier, Paquin had crawled into Jimmy Francis's sleeping bag and molested him." *This is a pattern! It's the same stuff he pulled on me!*

Reading the story brought memories of sitting in the pew at Jimmy's funeral, watching Paquin preside. I remembered glaring at him with silent hatred, thinking that he was probably still drunk behind that wheel. And now I knew for certain! Anger surged through me. I wanted to hit something, kick something, or just scream. I couldn't take it anymore! *They all knew! And these guys were allowed to carry on, without an ounce of concern for the lives that would be ruined. They were protecting pedophile priests. How many more undocumented cases were going to come up? How many more stories like mine were out there, yet to be told? No! What's done is done! Put on your game face! Put down the newspaper! And go to work! You can handle this. You're above it all.*

I pulled myself together, hopped into my car, and headed up 95, but I couldn't get this one out of my mind. I kept flashing back to that morning when I woke up and learned that Jimmy died. I pictured the wake and the line stretching for blocks. I thought about Father Paquin and how he used his position to establish himself as a respected figure of authority. It was like he had diplomatic immunity. I began to think that I had unfinished business. Like I started a journey in a former life, but never finished it. It was a pressing urge to do something, to do *anything*, but I didn't know what it was that I was supposed to be doing.

Tears flowed from underneath my sunglasses as I drove north. I lifted my coffee cup from its holder to take a swig, but I couldn't steady the coffee, my hand was shaking too violently. I was lost in the past while trying to drive into the future, and yet it seemed like I couldn't go forward unless I went back. It was confusing. I didn't know which way I was going. I snapped the wheel. Crossing several lanes of traffic, I darted for the exit. My tires squealed. It was like someone else was steering the car toward Haverhill. One part of me was screaming to get back to work, and the other part, now in control, was forcing me to find an answer, or to do something about the Catholic Church. I had to head back to St. John the Baptist, to where it all began. *Am I finally going to burn the church down?*

I approached St. John the Baptist and parked across the street next to the brick wall of the Haverhill stadium. I was now face-to-face with a place I hadn't seen in twenty years. Tears streamed, and I began to yell, "What the hell do you want from me? Why are you in my head? Just leave me alone! You and I have an understanding, you go your way and do your thing, and I'll go my way and do mine! Get it, you bastard? None of this is my fault! None of this is my problem! It's your mess, you made it happen, you clean it up! I don't want any part of it! And I don't want you in my life!"... I don't know how long I sat there after that with my eyes closed, resting my forehead on the steering wheel, but when I reached for my coffee, it was cold.

I called in sick and drove the streets of my old neighborhood looking for clues as to where it all went wrong. Perhaps there was something I would see, something that would spark my memory and help me make sense of it all. But no matter where I drove, and what I saw, I couldn't find any answers to the questions besieging me.

11. TWO JOBS

I started devoting more and more time to keeping up with the crisis. At work, I found myself clipping and printing out every article I could find, stuffing folders and keeping three-ring binders. Soon, several drawers in my desk were devoted to my research on the crisis. At the same time, I got frustrated with myself for devoting time to this madness. One part of me was telling me to get back to work, while the other part would not let me turn away from the crisis. What bothered me the most was that the Archdiocese of Boston, and in particular Cardinal Law, knew that there were sexual molesters, serial rapists, in their ranks, and yet they chose to protect the reputation of their church over the safety of its children.

Day after day, the *Globe* revealed the names of more pedophile priests. Night after night, the local TV stations interviewed the victims. By the end of April, it was clear that there were thousands of hidden victims and hundreds of abusive priests who had been caught and transferred, and that the church was fighting the release of even more documents. This was when it all collapsed on me. It came out of nowhere. It was like I was stuck underwater, clawing my way to the surface. My lungs felt like they were going to explode, but my air came back when I decided to attend one of those Voice of the Faithful (VOTF) meetings that I had been reading about. I had decided that there might be something there that could help me understand why this was happening.

The drive from Portsmouth to Newton-Wellesley was dark. The parking lot of St. John's was packed. *Wow! This can't all be for Voice of the Faithful!* I drove down a side street and found a spot. It was a cold night. I really didn't want to walk. *Just turn on the car and get out of here! What the hell are you doing? Look what this is doing to you! You're psychotic, a certifiable schizophrenic!* I sat in the car for several minutes, gripping the steering wheel and gnashing my teeth. *Why waste all the time and gas it took to get here, though?* I stepped on the sidewalk, slammed the car door, and started toward the basement. Along the way, my body turned to stone. Every muscle tensed up. I started to breathe heavily. After a few minutes, I arrived. I paused, then, fighting off tremors, took a step. I was easily the youngest person in the room. I was wearing a long, black leather trench coat, black shoes, dark dress pants, and a button-down collar. I thought I must have looked like a hit man to them, and began to worry that they may think that I was sent to wipe them out.

The place was full of people yelling. I pushed my way along the outer perimeter and found a spot along the back wall. Worried that someone would recognize me, I just froze there. I hardly moved. I was trying to control my breathing but was hyperventilating underneath my game face. I surveyed the scene.

The room was shoulder to shoulder with people mainly in their sixties and seventies. Some were listening, some were shouting, others were crying. On the stage, someone from VOTF was trying to get control of the room when a small thin lady with long, scraggly hair in the crowd took over. She was yelling wildly, like an insane person, holding up what seemed to be a large, novelty dollar bill with Cardinal Law's face on it. She was calling for justice, for the perpetrators to go to jail. She stormed the stage waving her prop, flailing, and babbling. The person from VOTF, who was trying to keep things in control, looked confused and embarrassed, but also exhibited a "here we go again" look. After about 30 seconds or so, a young man with blond hair, the only other young man I saw besides myself, took the screaming woman by the waist and escorted her off the stage and out the door. The crowd was agitated. The woman on the stage continued to try to calm the room. *What a bunch of nuts! These folks are all crazy, and this is a colossal waste of my time!*

Ungluing my back from the rear wall, I made my way along the perimeter and out the door. A sense of relief fell over me. *You came, you checked it out, and you found a bunch of lunatics. Now, you can go home and forget about all about it!* I walked back to the car, fired it up, and headed for a Dunkin' Donuts.

12. CALLING ME BACK

But, as insane as that meeting was, there was something about being a part of that crowd that comforted me. What was my connection to these crazies? What was it about the yelling, screaming, and crying that made me want to go back? What would people say if they knew I went to a VOTF meeting? It wouldn't add up to them. The more I fought it, the more it fought me.

But what the hell was "it" that was making me want to go these meetings? Was "it" God, the Holy Spirit, or a 15-year-old me? One thing was certain, traveling to St. John the Baptist in Haverhill to yell at it from across the street, or swearing at God to leave me alone, was not helping.

It took several weeks, but eventually I went back. I explained to my wife that I was, "Trying to find some freelance PR work on the side," but I was pissed off at myself for going back to Newton-Wellesley. It was another chilly April evening. I again entered wearing my long black leather coat and keenly pressed pants. This time, the event was moved to an adjacent hall. Their numbers had significantly grown. Standing in the doorway, I surveyed the crowd again, looking for recognizable faces. After not seeing anyone I knew, I entered and made my way around the perimeter to the wall. Again, every muscle in my body was tense while my heart pounded so hard that it echoed. I pressed my back tightly against the wall, clenched my teeth, and gazed toward the front.

This meeting was more structured. The members were more in control. I noticed several people in front of me holding folders stuffed with newspaper clippings and documents. *My God! Other people have been keeping files and documents just like me. I'm not alone in my madness.*

I sat there and watched as people were invited up front to tell their stories. I heard of how people they knew were abused, and about how they were once friendly with accused clergy members. But, nothing affected me until the stories from victims themselves were told.

One man stepped up and took the microphone. He was in his fifties or sixties, had thinning hair and was slightly overweight. As he began to tell his story of being abused by a trusted member of the clergy, I felt the air surrounding me tighten on my body. I felt like I was being vacuum packed. As he continued, my heart pounded. I shoved my hands into my pockets so that no one would see my fists. My fingernails dug deep into my palms.

Suddenly, the man's voice cracked, deep breaths replaced the words he was trying to convey, and he broke down sobbing. Then people approached him and laid their hands upon him. The room got hot. All the air was removed. *I have got to get out of here. I can't take this!*

I looked to retrace my steps to the exit, but people had filled the hall, blocking my path. I stood there, frozen, trapped with my back against the wall. I closed my eyes and took deep breaths. In the darkness, I began to hear a different tone, and when I opened my eyes, I could see that everyone had started to pray. There was something soothing about it. People were crying and holding hands.

These people were giving this man something he needed--something the church had taken from him many years ago. He walked off the stage, welcomed into more embraces. He was not alone, he was with family, with those who understood his pain and were willing to address it. This is where the church had failed. Instead of embracing the victims, offering healing and comfort, the church tried to expunge their existence. The church sent lawyers with hush money and gag orders. I stayed for a bit, and then left before it was over.

13. VEGAS

In May, my start-up displayed its software at the tech industry's largest trade show in Vegas. It was our chance to demonstrate that we could make it. There had been skepticism due to the recent report on the accounting errors. Customers weren't sure if we were going to be around for much longer. Damage control was needed, and. I was up for the challenge. My company put me up at the Venetian hotel, where gondolas floated under a replica of the Rialto Bridge. My room overlooked the Vegas strip. *Now this is more like it, just what I need to get my mind off this abuse nonsense.*

The morning of the trade show, I got up early, put on my dark blue suit, white collared button-down shirt, and red tie, and went to the floor to check out the booth. I had a day full of press meetings scheduled, and I was eager to get moving. It wasn't long before I was in the thick of it, hustling back and forth between meetings and greeting customers. I was engaged. It took my mind off of the Catholic stuff. The day flew. Everything went smoothly. I left the show with a smile, went to a few parties, and then retired early to my room.

The first few days went great, as my company was getting good press coverage. And then on the third night, I went to my room after the show, hung up my suit and checked my e-mail. A non-work related e-mail caught my attention, the subject: "Paquin Arrested."

It was a *Boston Globe* story about how Reverend Shanley's bail was set for $750,000, and it was about how Father Paquin had been arrested too, at his Malden apartment earlier that day. He was being charged with one count of rape of a child under 16. The *Globe* reported that, "Essex District Attorney, Kevin Burke, said the charge against Paquin involved at least 50 incidents with a young boy between 1990 and 1992 in Massachusetts, New Hampshire, and Maine. The first incident took place when the boy was 12. Paquin, now 59, admitted that he molested minors." The article also said "he was removed from active ministry in 1990 by the Boston archdiocese, which paid settlements to at least four of his victims, and that he was laicized in 2000.

Like a siege engine breaking a castle's wall, Vegas had been breached. A wave of anxiety rushed through me. I was happy Paquin was arrested but pissed off at myself for not being the one to do it. My hands trembled, and my eyes filled with tears.

I felt rage as I read on. "Cardinal Law, along with five bishops who served under him at various times, is accused in several civil lawsuits of negligence for transferring a known priest pedophile, John J. Geoghan, to a new parish in 1984, and allowing him to remain there for another eight years. Law's testimony is slated to begin at 9 a.m. The deposition will be closed to the press and public, but videotaped by the court in case Law is not available for a future trial. Judge Constance M. Sweeney said she accelerated the date of the deposition, rejecting a request by Law's attorney that he be given the standard seven-day notice, because of her concerns that Law might leave for Rome if the proceeding was further delayed."

I screamed across the Vegas strip, "Law can escape justice by hiding out in Rome! This is not right!" I paced around the room like a mad man, moving rapidly from the office area to sleeping area. My energy needed an outlet. I thought about all the missed opportunities to bring Paquin to justice, missed because I did not want to get involved. I also thought of the good work VOTF was doing to help victims of sexual abuse. That's when I decided to get involved but in what capacity? I did not know. I just knew that had to get involved.

There was a crumpled VOTF flyer stuffed in my briefcase. At the bottom was an e-mail address. I began typing, offering my skills as a seasoned PR practitioner. The e-mail was short. I did not want to oversell myself, just offer to help in any way I could, but I couldn't send it. I paused, contemplating what I was about to do. I thought about the risks, and what people who knew me might say. I thought about my family and my wife, I thought about all those I let down by remaining silent instead of bringing Paquin to justice, and mostly I thought about Cardinal Law escaping to Rome for the rest of his life. Then I hit send.

The lights on the strip began to illuminate the scene below my window. I walked over and gazed down in silence. My eyes were watery. *What am I becoming, and why can't I control it?* I noticed several stars fighting the neon from below, and I thought of Janis. Back in '98, I wanted to do something special for her, so I named a star "Mike Loves Janis," at the International Star Registry. I knew it was corny, but there was something cool about it. I knew the general direction our star was in, so I looked in that area and thought of Janis… and of our marriage less than a year earlier… and about our honeymoon in Italy, and about how I asked her to marry me right here at the Rio in Vegas. *I'm sorry. I'm not who you thought I was. I'm just a coward. Help me get through this. Help me find my way.*

I didn't go out to any parties that night. I ordered room service and sat in dark silence.

The rest of the show went as planned; except that my colleagues started asking me why I wasn't going out to the parties. I blamed my absence on needing to catch up with work. The Monday following the show, I was back at home. I rationalized reaching out to VOTF as just me being tired. After returning from a dinner celebrating my birthday, I sat down to scan my e-mails before heading to bed and noticed a return note from VOTF.

After telling myself that contacting them had been a bad dream, that e-mail was an awakening. I wasn't sure if I should respond. I wrestled. Part of me was angry for even considering returning it; the other part was pulling me to do something about the crisis. And, lately, the part pulling toward the crisis was stronger; so, I sent an e-mail back.

Days later, I was invited to the next meeting at St. John's by a woman named Svea. On my way, I was thinking, *I can get through this. I did work with The Commission on Presidential Debates in 2000. How bad can the press here be?* When I arrived, I was astonished. The place was even more packed than the last time. The meetings had now spilled into two halls. And adding to the anarchy were four or five broadcast trucks parked outside the church. I mustered up my courage and headed for the doors.

Crowds were coming in and out of the doorways leading to the school and church. I decided to enter the church to begin my search for Svea. I pushed through the crowd to find someone—anyone—who looked like they were in charge. I made my way up to the stage and grabbed the first person that seemed like they knew something. "Excuse me; do you know where Svea Fraser is?" I asked a gray-haired gentleman. He looked at me for a few seconds… and then, "No," was all he said, as he pushed his way to the stage. I got the feeling he didn't trust me. I thought I looked out of place, again—younger than most folks, and the only person with a leather trench coat. I went up to an elderly woman who was carrying pamphlets.

"Excuse me," I had said a bit more assertively. "Svea asked me to meet her here. Do you know where I may find her?" She, too, looked at me skeptically but paused and then told me she was in the school building, across the parking lot.

"Okay, then I'll just…" but before I could finish my sentence, she vanished into the crowd. "Thanks for your help," I said, under my breath. *Do I have "Asshole" written on my forehead?* I pushed my way through the crowd and headed for the door. I could not get over how many folks were in there. It made me uneasy. But no matter, time to get your game face on! I crossed the parking lot and headed for the school. On my way, I passed several satellite trucks: ABC, NBC, CBS, and NECN. *Wow! Is the pope here?* I joined a steady stream of people filing in through the school doorway and then found myself in a large hall. I noticed some literature on a table. I picked up some pamphlets, then, just as I had done the first two times, I pressed my back against the wall, took a deep breath, and surveyed the room.

It was a massive group that had filled the hall. Six individuals were sitting in folding chairs on the stage. I looked for someone that seemed to be an organizer on the floor. I spotted an old lady carrying Styrofoam cups. "Excuse me, Svea asked me to meet her here. Do you know where I can find her?

The lady pointed to a thin woman with short gray hair up on the stage, "She's up there."

"The tall, slender one?" I asked.

"Yes. Who are you?" she inquired.

"My name is Mike. I was trading e-mails with Svea about helping with the press.

"Great, you came at the right time." Then she continued on her way.

I made my way closer to the stage and waited for Svea to come down. Watching her, I noticed that she had elegance and poise that seemed to come from a forgotten era. As she made her way off the stage, she fielded questions from all directions. I waited for the right moment. Seeing a break, I moved in, "Svea?" I asked even though I was certain that it was her.

"Yes, may I help you?" she said in a soft and charming voice, extending a hand.

"I'm Mike Emerton. We traded e-mails about helping Voice of the Faithful with the press."

Svea grabbed my hand warmly, "Great!" she said, looking right into my eyes. "We can really use your help."

She then looked around the room and started pointing, "That guy over there is with *People Magazine*. He is looking for James Muller to interview. When he is done speaking with the *New York Times*, over there, make sure he speaks with them."

"Okay," I said.

She continued, "The BBC is just over there in the corner. Go talk to that guy in the white shirt, he's been trying to grab me for a while. And if you look over here..." I tried to follow as she pointed. I couldn't believe the press they had. Frantically, I tried to memorize faces as she pointed them out. Svea went on, "Over there you'll find several local news stations that need some help as well. I think they're looking for some victims to speak with, but be careful! Some folks just don't want to talk. There's also another publication running around here that claims they're from Ireland. See if you can find out who they are, and with whom they want to speak." My head was dizzy trying to follow her finger. "Okay, I... I have it! Who can I use for spokespeople?"

Svea quickly motioned to several people on stage, "That's Paul Baier, you can use him. Over there is Jim Post, and over there is Mary Scanlon, they're very good spokespeople. I've got to get going, but I'll be around, just come find me."

I blinked, and she was gone. I tried to digest what she told me. Not since the Commission on Presidential Debates had I ever seen such a group of top tier press assembled in one place. I wasn't sure where to start. The first thing I could remember was that People Magazine had a request to speak with James Muller. I walked up and introduced myself, "I am Mike Emerton. I'm helping Voice of the Faithful with PR. Is there anything I can do for you?" The reporter from People Magazine was agitated.

He looked at me and started to unload, "I've been waiting here for over an hour to speak with James Muller! I was told I could interview him tonight! I have not been able to get a hold of him. Get him over here!"

"Okay, I'll see what I can do, just hang on," I said, and I rushed over to the stage to find James Muller. On the way, I bumped into the reporter from the *New York Times*, who had some follow-up questions. I stopped to see if I could help her. "Hi, my name is Mike Emerton, and I'm helping Voice of the Faithful with PR. How can I help you?"

She turned around and fired questions at me, "Exactly when was the group formed? How many people are in the group? How many victims are in the group? Can I talk to some victims? I heard there was going to be a big meeting at the Hynes Convention Center, can you tell me a little bit about that?" Then she clicked her pen and pressed it against her notebook.

I stared at her. Frozen, I delivered the standard PR reply for when you don't have the answers, "Those are all great questions! Let me find you someone that can answer them better than I can."

She shook her head and said, "No, I'll find someone myself who can give me the answers! I'm on deadline! I have to get this story filed."

"Okay. I'll see if I can help right way!" I went off to find someone that could help her. On my way, I recognized James Muller talking to a small group of people. I entered with a quick introduction, "Hi James, my name is Mike Emerton, and I have been trading e-mails with Svea regarding helping you folks with PR. I was just speaking with People Magazine over there, and these guys really need to speak with you right away." I pointed across the room towards the reporter from People, who noticed me pointing at him.

"Hi, Mike! Glad to meet you," James said. "I'm really glad you're here to help. Svea let me know you were coming. I know People Magazine has been waiting. I just haven't been able to get to them."

"No worries. Do you have time to speak with them, now?" I asked.

"Yes," James replied, and together we started walking towards the reporter who kept his eye on me. I flashed him a quick thumbs up. He was pleased to see we were heading his way, and then a reporter from the BBC, with a cameraman, jumped in front of us to speak with James, and pulled him into a hallway. I could feel the cold stare from People Magazine on my back. I turned and held my index finger up, "Just one moment!" He was not pleased.

On my way to find James, again, the *New York Times* reporter ran into me and asked if I found anyone yet who could answer her questions. I took a step back to establish my personal space and said, "I'm on it. Just give me a couple minutes. I have James Muller right here, and you're next, after People." She shook her head and went off into the crowd.

Because James was now occupied in the hallway with the BBC, I decided this was a good time to go grab People Magazine and line them up behind the BBC. On my way over to People, a reporter from one of the local Boston stations grabbed me and requested an interview with James. "Okay, I'll see what I can do." Then I went off to get the reporter from People.

The entire evening went this way. I bounced back and forth from one reporter to another, trying to figure out how I could help them. But I was lost! I didn't know anything about VOTF. I didn't know the principal players or the key messages. It was my own fault. I threw myself right into it without thinking. The reporters that I was trying to help grew frustrated. After a while, they ignored me.

As I was making my way through the crowd looking for a VOTF spokesperson, I heard a photographer say, "Isn't that one of their PR people?"

"Yeah," said a reporter. "But he's a doofus and totally useless. He doesn't know a thing!"

This was said loud enough for me to hear. I heard something snap in my head, like the sound of a board cracking. I stood there staring at the reporter. Then all the noise in the room stopped. It was silent, yet clearly abuzz with conversation. I had never had a member of the press exhibit hostility toward me, and he was right! I was useless, and in way over my head!

But I pressed on. At the end of the evening, I was exhausted and felt defeated. My face was numb. I saw Svea walking out of the hall, "I did the best I could," I said. "But I don't know how much good it did."

"You did just fine. Thank you so much for all your help." Then she handed me a flyer and said, "We are having a steering committee meeting on May 23rd, can you make it? Part of what we're going to be speaking about is the press."

I didn't know what to say. I was stunned. I meekly took the flyer, looked at her with half a smile and said, "I'll send you an e-mail to let you know. I think I'm busy that evening, though." I turned and walked out of the hall. I felt dizzy and weak. I walked to the end of the parking lot, crossed the road, and took a seat on a stone wall across the street. Lights illuminated St. John's. I looked up and saw the media trucks shining their lights on the correspondents doing broadcasts. I watched their figures glow as they reported. I felt hollow. I was a shell. Everything I thought I knew about myself was had evaporated. It was as if I was an empty tin can on the sidewalk. I hung my head and sobbed like never before. Decades poured out. I didn't know where I was going anymore. The path that was clear had vanished. I began to feel cold. I wrapped my arms around my waist in an attempt to stay warm, but I couldn't, I shook so violently. Eventually, I stood up hoping no one saw that as I walked back to my car, trying all the way to stop shaking, so I'd be able to drive.

14. WHO AM I?

I was now a stranger in my own mind. I had the feeling that I was lost, but VOTF was providing direction. I arrived at the church late to the meeting that I told Svea I most likely could not attend, and I took a few minutes to collect myself in the parking lot. I could see the light on in the basement. There were at least 15 cars in the lot. I stepped out and walked toward the door. I paused, took a deep breath, and opened it.

Twenty people sat in metal folding chairs that formed a circle in the room. I stood in the doorway. Everybody turned to look at me. People sitting with their backs to me nudged their chairs so that they could see. The metal groaned and squeaked against the cement floor. I felt a bit silly standing there.

Then I recognized James Muller, the cardiologist and Noble Peace Prize winner. Also in attendance were Susan Troy, who possesses a Masters of Divinity; Jim Post, a professor with an MBA, Ph.D. and law degree; Paul Baier, one of the younger members, an entrepreneur and Harvard Business School graduate; Bill Fallon, an accomplished businessman who sat with his wife Cathy, an official at Brandeis University, and Steve Krueger, who was appointed to the Archdiocesan Pastoral Council. I had an awful pain in my stomach. *You are way out of your league here, little boy.* I took a deep breath and scanned the room.

On the far side of the circle, I noticed Svea looking at me and smiling. She patted the empty folding chair next to her. *How did she know that I would even be coming? I didn't make the decision until the last minute.* I took another deep breath. I could feel everybody's eyes upon me as I made the long journey to the empty seat. When I reached the seat, Svea said, "I knew you would come."

My head was spinning. I tried to form a smile. As I took my seat, Svea introduced me as a new member and told the group that I would be helping with the media. I introduced myself, told about my PR career, and then shut my mouth. I didn't want to sound foolish.

As I listened, it became clear to me that this was a group of concerned Catholics that wanted to help the church get through this crisis. There was a sense of excitement as they tossed around ideas, but I didn't know what I had to offer. I was a high-tech PR guy. These folks were all steeped in Catholicism, something I dropped a long time ago. As I listened, I thought I had nothing to offer, and every time my doubts hit a crescendo, Svea smiled at me, and they went away. What she saw in me, I still don't know.

They talked about their love for the church and how to support victims. They talked about an open letter to the bishop explaining their mission. Then the conversation turned to the press, and an op-ed piece in the *New York Times*. I took notes.

The part I found most interesting was the briefing Mary Scanlon, James Muller, and Steve Krueger gave about a meeting they had with Bishop Edyvean, Cardinal Law's right-hand man. Going into this meeting, Mary, James, and Steve felt the press had been painting them as a positive organization. They were taking comfort in the fact that they had never taken a position on such controversial issues as ordination for women, birth control, or married priests. The Boston Archdiocese, however, had a very different view.

Bishop Edyvean had been calling parish priests telling them not to allow VOTF groups to meet in their parishes. "According to canon law, if the bishop informs you to not engage in what he believes to be a subversive activity, he must put it in writing," Steve said.

"I have heard that they will not resort to that method since they are afraid the press will get a copy," replied Svea.

It seemed that the meeting with the bishop was tense. VOTF had been accused of calling for Cardinal Law's resignation, and they were chastised for it. It seemed that a Father O'Connell, who was also in attendance, blew a gasket when Steve Krueger let him know the group had established a fund to help raise money to support the dwindling Cardinal's Appeal.

James Muller explained, "Father O'Connell said that the importance of the right relationship between the archbishop and his church took primacy over funding the programs and ministries of the archdiocese. To clearly illustrate this, he reached up with his left hand, held it above his head, and said, 'Principle is up here!' Then he reached down with his right hand, holding it way below the level of the table, and said, 'Money is down here!'"

As a result of the meeting with Bishop Edyvean, VOTF, and the bishop agreed to issue a joint statement to the press. Shortly after the meeting, Mary received a phone call from a reporter seeking a comment. The reporter quoted from a statement that was issued by the archdiocese that said that VOTF had agreed to operate only under Cardinal Law's direction. But that was never said. So much for joint efforts!

Several days later, the *Globe* ran a story titled, "Records Show Law Reassigned Paquin After Settlements." It seemed "Law had reinstated Paquin to priestly duties as recently as 1998, despite numerous complaints of molestation against him, and substantial monetary settlements to his victims. Between 1990 and 1996, there were 13 complaints to the archdiocese alleging sexual misbehavior by Paquin." The story went on in grim detail to explain how "Paquin plied all his victims with gifts and liquor before molesting and/or raping them. His behavior was found to be so repugnant, and the pattern of abuse so clear, that a church review board, and a top deputy to Law, urged Paquin be dismissed from the priesthood." Later, though, they changed their minds and said that he should be given a second chance. The documents which the *Globe* had gotten a hold of showed that "Law's 1998 decision allowing Paquin to return to duty as a chaplain at a hospital in Cambridge was made at the urging of another priest, who had himself been removed from parish work for allegations of child molestation."

Learning for a fact that Cardinal Law reassigned Paquin while knowing he was a sexual predator, and now seeing firsthand how he was trying to quash this voice of concern from the people in the pews, gave me a new resolve.

15. MISSION

By June, I had become more comfortable with VOTF's goals and was able to enforce key messages in the Boston area press. The messages were simple. VOTF:

1. Supports survivors of clergy sexual abuse.
2. Supports priests of integrity.
3. Pushes for structural change within the church.

Most people didn't have a problem with the first two; it was the third one calling for change that frightened them. This goal had to be carefully explained. The group wanted it understood that they wished to work with members of the church to establish a more open and honest dialog, but the archdiocese had labeled them, "dissidents."

Whenever I met journalists, they always had the same question, "Are you a survivor of clergy sexual abuse?" I always delivered the same answer, which I delivered to the VOTF members as well, "No, I'm just a concerned Catholic trying to help out where I can."

It was not part of my mission to become the story, but rather to be a conduit for it. A PR person's job is to not be in the spotlight, but to spotlight the product.

The eighteen-hour workdays became normal. My work phone was constantly ringing with press inquiries for VOTF. I shut myself in my office. I was putting far more time into VOTF than I was pitching the latest tech gizmos, but that didn't matter because now the tech world was second, and VOTF was first. My parent company's "cooking of the books" crisis in Asia had done irreparable damage to the spin-off company. We all knew it was about to go under and were waiting for pink slips. The press and the customers knew, as well. There was no getting around it. The ship had sunk. My co-workers began polishing resumes and using personal days. This was all fine by me because the impending doom was exactly the distraction I needed in order to conduct my VOTF business during work hours.

Another steering committee meeting was held on a Sunday that June on a Sunday another steering committee meeting was held. On the surface, it seemed to be routine, but in reality, it was another one of those moments that would affect my life forever. This meeting was like all the others, held in a big room with lots of noisy metal chairs formed into in a ring, but this one was about establishing the governance of the group. James Muller had a PowerPoint presentation outlining a one-year tactical plan. VOTF was transforming itself from an idea into an organization. The amount of thought and work that went into this was mind-boggling to me. These people had full-time jobs. They were doctors, lawyers, professors, financial advisors, and more. *How do they find time for their day jobs and families?*

It was amazing to witness this movement. I sat in the circle and stayed quiet, keeping busy by taking notes. After a while, the conversation turned to the Dallas Bishops' Conference in July. The group discussed which bishops and priests they could turn to for support, and what the press statement should encompass. It was also discussed which members would be sent to gather information. It was at this point that I opened my mouth, "Excuse me. But I think Voice of the Faithful should have a bigger presence. I don't think going down to collect info and monitoring the situation is what you want to be doing.

Everyone's eyes focused on me. Blood rushed to my face. I continued to speak, "I think the Dallas bishops' conference is an outstanding opportunity for Voice of the Faithful to hold a press conference of its own to let the entire world know what you think. Think about it! Every major news organization from around the world will be descending on this event, and you will have an opportunity to address them, one-on-one, and become a go-to organization for comments.

A gentleman to my right, named Terry, stood up informed the group that this was a bad idea. He thought we should just go to Dallas, gather information, and report back.

"You're wrong," I said. "This is your opportunity to set the tone for the press, so they can take your questions to the bishops, and force them to address these questions that they refuse to address. You have already established incredible and positive momentum with the press.

"You can take that momentum and leverage it, bring it up to a whole new level. You could hold a press conference before the bishops meet. That way, you can convey the laity's voice and what you want to see the bishops accomplish behind those closed doors."

Terry, again, stressed that this was not a good idea, and I found myself blurting out more ideas. "This will be your time to take control and issue statements for the bishops to address, rather than Voice of the Faithful always having to address statements from the bishops."

The whole conversation between Terry and I probably lasted about four minutes, but it felt like an eternity. People's eyes were going back and forth between us. Every muscle I had began to quiver.

James Muller was the definitive voice, and he acknowledged that holding a press conference was a good idea and said, "Mike, we need you to go down, set it all up, and run the show."

My face turned white. I was in shock. *Did I just hear what I thought? I'm going to run a press conference in Dallas? There is no way in hell I am going to do that! And, there is no way in hell I can say, "No," now, either.*

"That's fine, I'll get this done for you," I said, but I knew that I couldn't just disappear from work and family and take off for Dallas. What would I tell everybody? Thinking about it made my stomach sick, and my breathing labored. My palms began to sweat. I sat down and started looking for a way to get out. I was thinking of running, and not ever coming back. *You'll never see these people again.* I waited for the conversation to move off the topic of Dallas, and then I excused myself, stating that I needed to go to the bathroom.

I left the room and walked down a long hallway looking for someplace to be alone, to break down. I couldn't find a men's room, but I saw a little room that seemed like it was set up as a small praying area. I looked behind me to make sure no one was looking, and then ducked into the room and closed the door.

I sat in a wooden chair in the corner. I was hyperventilating. I couldn't catch my breath. I folded my hands together and leaned my face into them. I didn't know what to do. I couldn't tell them "No," but neither could I couldn't explain to my family, friends and work colleagues why I thought that it was so crucial for me to go to Dallas. *What are you doing? Why are you putting yourself into this position?*

I wasn't sure how long I had been sitting in that room, but I knew that it was longer than a person would normally take to go to the bathroom. I took a deep breath and headed back to the group. Before entering, I took my cell phone out of my pocket and placed it against my ear to make it look as if I had an important call. Then I put it back in my pocket, for all to see, as I reentered the room and sat down.

After several more hours, the group adjourned. I now had a lot of work to do. I needed to get the press room reserved, invitations sent out, talking points created, and, most importantly, I needed to figure out how I was going to disappear for three days without calling attention to myself.

16. RESPONSE

As June went on, I had to get my spokespeople in line. Press inquiries were picking up. Forced by the overwhelming public outrage, the bishops agreed to produce a document intended to strengthen the church's commitment to preventing the sexual abuse of minors by clergy and other church workers. They stated that they would be gathering in Dallas in July to create a special charter to help them see that sexual abuse was wrong.

I couldn't wrap my head around it. How can these people act in such opposition to what they preach? People for generations had put their faith in a church that had been harboring criminals. The laity didn't matter; they were to keep their mouths shut and keep the funds flowing. *Don't ask questions, do what you are told.* It occurred to me, however, that there were passionate, good priests, who were doing their jobs honestly, and these good priests were now finding themselves in the unfortunate situation of being part of a corrupt organization.

I booked a meeting room in Dallas in the same hotel the bishops were meeting in. I just needed a large empty room, one podium, microphone, speakers, and a media box.

Once I put out the media alert stating that VOTF would be conducting a press conference before the Bishops' Conference, my cell phone never stopped ringing: *ABC News*, *CBS Evening News with Dan Rather*, the *Providence Rhode Island Journal*, *Dallas Morning News*, *Boston Globe*, NBC, BBC World Radio, AP, Reuters, MSNBC, *Newsweek*, Tokyo Broadcasting—"Hello Mr. Emerton, this is Yuki. Thank you for granting my request for an interview."

This was the big time. The message had to be crisp, clean, and consistent. I struggled as I tried to match the right personality with the right press. It was difficult because I was also trying to conduct my day job, too. The VOTF work spilled into my evenings and weekends. The pressure was mounting, consuming my life, and there was no stopping it.

Shortly before the conference, Janis got tickets to see Riverdance at Boston's Wang Center. The show was billed as a theatrical event of traditional Irish step dancing. We invited my mother and Janis' mother and stepfather. I had at least ten interviews still to line up. My mother looked at me and said, "You don't look like yourself. Is everything all right?"

"Yes, I'm fine," I replied. "I just have a lot on my mind."

"Well, try to relax. This will be fun."

I thought, "Yeah. She's right. I need a show to take my mind off of things." When the show began, I tried to enjoy it, but I had too much to worry about. I couldn't get my mind off of VOTF matters. The curtain went up, and a long line of dancers appeared wearing red and black sequenced costumes.

"This is nice," I thought.

But the loud shoe tapping and the thundering drum quickly made me anxious. The whole line of dancers was bobbing up and down with their feet wildly tapping the stage floor. My eyes widened, my pulse quickened. Every foot tap and every beat of the drum seemed to increase the pressure in my head and tighten the grip around my heart. I closed my eyes, but the drumbeat, joined by the fiddles, and the foot tapping, kept increasing in speed and volume. The music penetrated my body. I shut my eyes. It got louder, the tapping stronger. I looked for the nearest exit.

My wife was caught up in the show and didn't seem to notice my predicament. The performers were picking up in intensity as they formed patterns on the stage. The drums and fiddles urged them to go faster. It was torture! I just focused on the exit door. I had to make a decision: I was either going to run or stay and have a mental breakdown. The shoes clapped wildly and the drums just beat on. I weighed my options: *If that's an emergency exit, the alarm will go off, the show will stop, and people will file out. If it's a door to the hallway, it will still make a scene. Maybe there's another door?* The strings screeched. The dancers formed an X and rotated clockwise. Boom! Boom! Boom! I closed my eyes, took a deep breath through my nose, and exhaled it from my mouth. I repeated that again and again until my heart rate slowed, and I got back some control. The tempo of the music calmed. I opened my eyes, looked over at my wife, and smiled.

17. GAME FACE

As the conference approached, I found myself constantly on the phone speaking to the press. Any time a bishop commented, or a new allegation of sexual abuse was brought to light, VOTF was sought for commentary. Our ultimate position was that the Catholic Church is not above the law. The Church must be held accountable, and given the abuse crisis, a request to change the church seemed simple. But, the bishops didn't get it because they were the ones who had been covering-up the abuse—they were complicit! It was truly absurd!

When I was immersed in the work, things didn't bother me, but if I slowed down, I began to feel anxious. Night was the worst. Sleep rarely stayed with me. I found myself staring at the ceiling. My mind kept churning. I was worried about pulling off the press conference. I was worried about what people would think of me. But mostly, I was worried that if I blew this one, then it was all over for VOTF. I couldn't relax. I couldn't calm down. I had about all I could take. I needed to tell someone what I was doing. I needed to speak to Janis, but there was a sense of pride in me that kept me from opening up to her. I knew, though, that if I didn't tell her, then I would surely have a breakdown.

So, on the morning of my flight to Dallas, I wrote my wife a letter. I left it on the kitchen table and walked out.

The letter read:

How do you begin a letter to the one you love to explain your own insanity? Perhaps, this is a start: The past six months have awakened feelings that I thought had long since been put to rest, something I dealt with decades ago and moved on. When I was asked if something happened with Father Paquin and said "No," that wasn't true.

When Father Paquin and I traveled to Canada, there was an evening when I got very drunk and passed out. I can't tell you exactly what happened, but I remember a strange look on his face when he asked me if I could remember anything. And I got a creepy feeling.

Then on a camping trip, he and I shared a tent. In the morning, he got touchy, and I got out of the tent. At that time, I filed it away as a strange circumstance. I haven't told anyone this.

Over the past six months, I have learned through the press that my circumstance is not an isolated one. What saddens me greatly is that my particular situation could have been prevented had Paquin been stopped in Methuen. It was the cover-up by the hierarchy that caused and allowed it to happen.

I wanted to tell you a thousand times, but I could never bring myself to say the words. This is a character flaw that my father had, and one that I received. My father was a man who could never speak of his feelings, or talk about his demons, whatever they were, and they consumed him in the end.

I must find a way to address my demons, or suffer my father's fate. That is why I have forced myself to take on this task. Perhaps, it's all part of a grand plan. At times, I feel driven and happy, other times as if I could crumble. I feel that I must do everything I can to shed light on this cover up and abuse, or I'll be as guilty as those who covered it up and did it.

I know it's a lot to ask you to understand when I cannot even explain it. The one truth I have left is you. Dallas will be the beginning of a long battle. VOTF is a good group of people, and I believe one that can make a change if I carry the message properly, and I have your love to guide me.

I love you always,

Mike

18. GOT A PLANE TO CATCH

About half way down Route 1, Janis called. We both broke down and cried as I drove. I assured her that I was okay and that I was doing the right thing. I told her that I couldn't explain my actions and that I was being driven to do what I was doing. I hated myself for putting her through this, but I had no choice. Janis listened and at the end of the conversation she urged me to contact my mother. I agreed that I would when the time was right.

As the Boston skyline came into view, our conversation ended. I wiped the tears from my eyes and took Exit 60. I didn't want to be doing it, but I couldn't turn away. I wanted my life back. I wanted easier times—I wanted those times when I knew what I was doing and where I was going.

I met Paul Baier at Boston's Logan Airport, and we boarded the flight to Dallas. He could tell that there was something wrong, and he kept pressing me for an answer. I decided to confide in him. I told him my story. A look of shock mixed with understanding came from his face as he listened. I pleaded with him to not tell anyone, to keep it a secret.

When we landed in Dallas, I checked my phone. There were at least 50 voicemails. I stuck my phone into my ear and started to jot down notes in a small red notebook while Paul drove to the hotel.

I was still returning phone calls and setting up meetings well after midnight. Paul was stretched out on his bed sending e-mails. Then he closed his laptop, looked at me, and said, "It's time to stop. You've been on the phone for hours."

"I just need to return several more calls; they are important," I replied.

Paul responded with, "You've got to take a break. You can't go on like this."

I nodded my head and began to jot down notes from another voicemail, but Paul was right. I was exhausted. I hadn't ever felt that tired. After I had returned my last message, I walked over to the window and gazed at the sky. I looked for our star, "Mike Loves Janis." I knew it was there, and that gave me a sense of comfort. The star, which represented my love for Janis, was my constant. Everything else had been turned upside down. Janis was my fixed point, and no matter where I was I could look up for the star.

Looking up, I wondered where this whole thing was going to take me, who would become, and if it would ever end. I then turned from the window, walked to my bed, put my head on the pillow, and stared at the ceiling.

A few hours later, I awoke and hopped into the shower. ABC was at 10 AM. I met the reporter in the lobby. She was a pretty, slender, woman with shoulder length blond hair. We had a brief discussion about VOTF as the microphone was being clipped to my shirt. There was a knot in my stomach and a lot of pressure inside. I thought about the letter I wrote to my wife, and the phone call I said that I would make to my mother. The lights illuminated, the camera turned on, and then she began her questioning.

"Are you an abuse victim?" She blurted out. Her eyes then focused on me.

Time just stopped. My answer to this question 100 times before was always, "No."

But this time was different. In a flash, I thought, "Will my family and friends see this? Will people treat me differently from now on? Am I making myself the story? It will look like I'm leveraging VOTF for personal gain! How will this affect the VOTF conference coming up?" My heart was racing, and the world was spinning.

"Yes," I replied.

And then all of a sudden… the only thing I could see was the reporter and the camera. The reporter continued, "Can you tell me about it?"

I took a breath, widened my eyes, "It was in the early 80's by Father Paquin," I began.

Tunnel vision began to set in, and every syllable was laborious. I wanted to say just enough to register that I had experienced the pain of the victims. As I continued, my body felt very cold and tightened up. My movements and mannerisms became robotic, and then it happened! All of a sudden I was looking down at the interview from the ceiling, and I saw how stupid I looked. *What are people going to think of you now? You're acting like an idiot for the entire world to see! You scared little boy, you really have come a long way haven't you? That's right! And you're throwing it all away! Fool!* A lifetime compressed into a minute that collapsed into a second that warped time.

Then it was over; the journalist finished her questions. I struggled to recall what I said, but I couldn't seem to piece it together. I picked up my phone and silently walked away from the interview. My voicemail was packed, but I couldn't deal with it. I needed to find a quiet place to call my mother. I exited the lobby and kept walking through hallways until I came to an exit that led to a plaza. I looked around to make sure that no one was in the area. It was clean. Everyone was busy with the hubbub in the lobby. I sat down on a bench and dialed my mother's home phone. My hands were shaking so badly that it took me several attempts to get the numbers correct. She picked up.

"Hello?"

"Hi, it's Mike."

"I did not expect you to be calling. What's up?

"I have something to tell you," I blurted out with a shaky voice.

"What's wrong? Are you all right?" she asked.

"Yes. But, remember when I said that nothing happened with Father Paquin? Well, that was not the true." My eyes filled, and my throat locked up. I could no longer talk.

"Mike! Are you there?"

I managed a mucus-filled, "Yes."

Hanging my head down, I unfurled a story that should have been told decades before. Then I attempted to explain why I was in Dallas. "I feel I need to be here, doing what I'm doing," I continued. "I can't explain it, but it needs to be done."

My mother was silent.

"I don't want to be like dad! He let everything fester inside until he died."

"You're not like your father," she immediately replied.

I choked up and could not speak.

"Are you there? Are you all right?!" she asked, again.

"Yes," was all I could manage to say.

"You're doing incredible things," she said.

"Thanks," I replied.

"I just want to see you come home safe so that I can look into your eyes," she told me.

Gulping back tears, I said, "You will. But right now, I have to conduct a press conference."

"Are you going to be okay to do that?" she inquired.

"I have to be, I have no choice," was my reply.

Taking a deep breath, I assured her that I would be okay and that we would talk again soon. I walked around the plaza to get my composure back. I reentered the hotel and made my way to the lobby. It was packed. Camera crews were running around everywhere; people were being interviewed. It was chaos. Before I stepped on the escalator, I adjusted the VOTF sign for our conference. As the escalator ascended, I turned around for a view of the lobby. *Things will never be the same again.*

19. THE CONFERENCE

The room was nothing fancy, but met the budget, and suited the needs. Podium, check! VOTF sign check! Microphone, media box, table with water, press kits check, and lots of space for cameras check! Everything was in place. I picked up a press kit to review the topics. I then called James Muller to have one last conversation before I took the podium. He informed me that Bishop Wilton Gregory, leader of the United States Conference of Catholic Bishops, had been quoted in *Time Magazine* as saying that the problems were a result of the hierarchy having too much power. James said that the laity now needed to organize to share that power. "It is often stated," he said "that the church is not a democracy, however, this Bishops' Conference is conducted with democratic principles. Voice of the Faithful should provide the same thing for the laity. The laity needs more involvement, we don't expect to decide on doctrine, but we do expect to help with administration." *That makes sense.*

As 2:00 PM approached, the press filed in. There were news outlets from all over the world. I greeted each member and made sure they grabbed a kit. Then it was time. Game face, check! I approached the podium with Paul Baier and Tanya Chermak at my side. Camera flashes went off; broadcast lights turned on, audio recorders closed in. All lenses and microphones were focused on me. I gazed out and thought, "This can't be happening!" But it was. "Ahem.

"Thank you for taking the time from your busy schedules to attend the Voice of the Faithful press conference in Dallas. If you have not already done so, please pick up a press kit on the back table. It has additional information regarding the topics we will be covering." I paused. My heart was racing, but everything seemed good, so I continued. "We represent Voice of the Faithful, a lay organization formed in the wake of the Catholic sexual abuse crisis and founded in the Boston area.

I then explained that VOTF was trying to work with the bishops to help find a quick and plausible solution to this crisis that we were attempting to sit down with them for open and honest dialog. But, in many parishes around the country, bishops were resisting the invitation to speak to their parishioners, and that made it look like they were trying to hide something. "All we are asked to do is pray, pay, and obey," I said. "We need a leveling of power."

I then explained how, in four short months, our membership had grown to 19,000, nationwide and announced that the group had reached an agreement in principle with the National Catholic Community Foundation (NCCF) to sponsor a charitable fund to support Catholic ministries in the Archdiocese of Boston. The initiative responded to the interests expressed by Catholic donors for greater accountability and transparency. A key feature was that all monies contributed were restricted to the direct costs of the charitable programs, not to the indirect ones. People were skeptical of giving money to the diocesan coffers, money that could be diverted to pay legal and settlement fees. VOTF wanted to establish this optional fund. The president of NCCF, called our agreement a "Landmark in the evolution of Catholic philanthropy in the United States," and emphasized how significant it was that it stemmed from the laity and involved lay management and oversight.

I then quoted a letter from one such donor: "I feel that the money I donate for good should go to the work that Jesus asked we carry out. I do not want my hard earned money being used to cover up the deeds of evil. My faith is in the many good lay people and priests that I have known in my lifetime. Those who have given so much of their time and efforts to spread God's kingdom on earth, deserve our support. I pray for the church that I have loved. May God guide and protect so that we may serve the Lord and the souls entrusted in our care."

In Cardinal Law's eyes, the fund was a big No, No. We received many comments from the archdiocese that it was absolutely unacceptable, and that VOTF had no business raising funds for Catholic ministries. But the annual Cardinal's Appeal was way down due to the scandal, and most Boston-area Catholics no longer trusted Law with their money.

I turned the microphone over to Paul, who spoke about how the church knew they had a pedophile problem since the report by Tom Doyle, and Ray Mouton was sent to the Vatican in 1985. He then went on to tell the story of how the Vatican thanked Doyle for that report by putting a "gag order" on him. Then Paul turned the microphone over to Tanya who spoke about the loss of moral leadership. I ended by mentioning the VOTF event on July 20 at Boston's Hynes Convention Center.

It was a success. VOTF was now firmly implanted on the national and international stage as a lay movement formed to help solve the Catholic Church's crisis. I had a true sense of accomplishment, but could not dwell on it for too long, as I had dozens of calls to make.

The rest of the conference was a waiting game. Everyone was waiting for the bishops to come out and say something. They were locked behind closed doors at the end of the hallway but had allowed CSPAN to cover some of the conference. The broadcast was shown on screens in the hotel's restaurant and bar area. That was where everyone, who wasn't a bishop, had gathered.

Law kept a low profile. His mistake of not reporting sexual abuse crimes to the authorities and sheltering pedophile priests was monumental. Journalists had been hounding him all year and were still at his heels, surrounding him like dogs on a stag as he walked through the lobby.

Heads turned and, even though he was being closed in upon, shouted at, and blocked, I couldn't help but admire his grace as he stopped to shake a hand. A true diplomat! As photographers whirled to get shots of the shake, it hit me. This was a setup! It was a photo-op that would show a smiling Cardinal Law, taking the time to touch the common folk.

I shook my head and opened up my laptop. A report by the *Dallas Morning News* had just been released saying that two-thirds of U.S. bishops had allowed accused priests to continue working with children. Everyone in the lobby was talking about it. Copies of the newspaper were all over the lobby. The pattern of cover-up went far beyond Boston. That was why the Pope had summoned the American cardinals to Rome in April. Now, with the world watching, and the crisis deepening, the bishops were behind closed doors drafting a policy—but it would not address their role in concealing or enabling it. Prosecutors around the country had begun examining the bishops' actions. The Vatican instructed them to not cooperate.

Meanwhile, polls revealed that most American Catholics believed that church leaders involved in cover-ups should resign. Four bishops had resigned already, after being accused of sexual misconduct. The *Dallas Morning News* investigation revealed that "at least 111 of the nation's 178 dioceses were headed by men who had protected accused priests, or other church figures—such as brothers in religious orders, candidates for the priesthood, teachers and youth group workers." This was not just a Boston problem blown out of proportion by the press, as the bishops asserted. It was a nationwide issue.

Then, all of a sudden, all the lounge area screens that were covering the conference behind the doors went black. Someone shouted, "The bishops are controlling the broadcast!" [Before the conference, the Boston Archdiocese had prohibited the *Globe* from covering live portions of it. It was a punishment for them having been the ones who pushed Judge Sweeny to break the seals, revealing the names of pedophile priests and those superiors who covered up for them.

The doors to the bishops' chambers opened, and everyone in the lounge rushed the conference room. It was madness as people jostled for position and shouted questions. A new policy was approved, and a statement was read:

The Catholic Church in the United States is in a very grave crisis, perhaps the gravest we have faced. This crisis is not about a lack of faith in God. In fact, those Catholics who live their faith actively day by day will tell you that their faith in God is not in jeopardy. It has indeed been tested by this crisis. But it is very much intact.

The crisis, in truth, is about a profound loss of confidence by the faithful in our leadership as shepherds, because of our failures in addressing the crime of the sexual abuse of children and young people by priests and church personnel.

Both what we have done or what we have failed to do contributed to the sexual abuse of children and young people by clergy and Church personnel. Moreover, our God-given duty as shepherds of the Lord's people holds us responsible and accountable to God and to the Church for the spiritual and moral health of all of God's children, especially those who are weak and most vulnerable. It is we who need to confess, and so we do.

We are the ones, whether through ignorance or lack of vigilance or, God forbid, with knowledge, who allowed priest abusers to remain in ministry and reassigned them to communities where they continued to abuse.

We are the ones who chose not to report the criminal actions of priests to the authorities because the law did not require this.

We are the ones who worried more about the possibility of scandal than bringing about the kind of openness that helps prevent abuse.

And we are the ones who, at times, responded to victims and their families as adversaries and not as suffering members of the Church.

The task that we bishops have before us these days in Dallas is enormous and daunting. We are called to put into place policies that will ensure the full protection of our children and young people and to bring an end to sexual abuse in the Church. This we will do.

> *Sadly, however, no decisions or policies that we make or put in place can save our children from human depravity. Our actions will have to be matched by an uncommon and persistent vigilance.*

Paul and I went outside to call the other VOTF members. On the way out, we noticed David and Mark, two founding members of the Survivors Network of those Abused by Priests (SNAP). We had been working closely with them over the last several months. They were literally the poster children of the Catholic Church's sexual abuse scandal. They were the ones at the protests carrying poster-sized pictures of themselves taken at the age that they were abused. The press had been following them throughout the scandal, and they had about thirty journalists around them as they walked down the sidewalk. Then they stopped. As they stopped to speak to the press, emotions took over. They just held each other and cried. Mark noticed Paul standing nearby and pulled him in to take over. Paul began to speak, but no one was listening. The cameras moved in on David and Mark. I pulled Paul's arm to get him out of the frame, "It's not our time. It's their time now," I said.

The following morning, I finished up my interviews and had started for the elevator when I noticed that Janis was calling. As I answered, the phone made several beeping noises, telling me the battery was about to die. "Hang on, Honey! I have to find the power cord; my phone is about to die." Next to the elevators there was a table with a lamp plugged into the wall. I followed the lamp cord to the outlet and plugged in my cell phone. "That's better," I informed her. What's up?

"I have a funny situation," she said.

"Lay it on me, I could use a laugh."

She said that she had woken up and found our cat, Bubba, staring and growling at the fireplace with her tail moving back and forth. It seemed a small bird had fallen down the chimney and was trapped in the fireplace behind the screen. The bird couldn't find its way past the damper, nor could it get by the screen. It huddled in the corner. Feathers littered the pit. The bird cowered and waited for the cat to devour it. Bubba hissed, showing his sharp teeth.

"What do I do?" asked Janis.

"I need a moment to process," I said. Then, I said, "Well, get Bubba out of the room first, that'll give the bird a break."

"Then what?" she asked.

"Maybe, try taking a towel, gently surround the bird, pick it up, bring it outside, and let it go."

"Okay. I'll try it.

"Let me know how you make out." We said goodbye.

A few minutes later, she called back. "It worked!"

The bird was free!

20. WE THE PEOPLE

The interview in Dallas about my abuse at the hands of Paquin was shown only in the Dallas area. I didn't see it. I didn't want to. I had done what I needed to do to relieve some of my pressure. Now I could focus on VOTF and keep the pressure where it should be, on Cardinal Law. I decided not to speak anymore about my abuse. I didn't want to become the story. "But then again," I thought, "if the press knew that I was a victim, it could lend credibility to the VOTF message." I weighed the options and decided it was best to stick to VOTF's messages.

Early in July, VOTF made an urgent request to hold a press conference at Boston's Faneuil Hall. It was to be held the day before the group's big convention at the Hynes Center. The theme was accountability from both church and state for survivors of clerical sexual abuse and was intended to raise awareness for the gathering at the Hynes Center. However, after our presence at the Bishops' Conference, and the way word was spreading through e-mails, we didn't have to work too hard for publicity anymore. VOTF had transformed. Elections for officers had been held, a board formed, and the group was growing by the thousands weekly. In parallel, Boston-area priests had organized what was called, the Priest's Forum, members of which joined our steering committee.

The Forum was meant to address the feelings of isolation and abandonment by the archdiocese the parish priests were having. They expressed a desire for this forum to serve as a professional association to overcome this separation, to commune, and to pick-up their spirits. In addition, they noted that this kind of association would become increasingly more important as their numbers decreased. Every year there were fewer and fewer priests.

At one of our meetings, Father Walter rose and said, "Coming together like this has been so exciting. While there have always been retreats held for us priests in the past, we were never really able to speak the truth at these things. What was missing was the very issues that Voice of the Faithful have raised, a discussion on the accountability of bishops, and what kind of a church we are going to be. And it's wonderful to see!"

Jim Post then said, "Voice of the Faithful is helping finish the work of Vatican II. And the time is right to explore a new way of being together, of developing trust between the hierarchy and the laity and the clergy, of taking risks, and of collaborating without apologies, without fear."

Father Walter, pointing his finger at the group, challenged VOTF to take action against the hierarchy, and said, "There is a difference between being deferential and being respectful."

Then a question was posed, "But how can we best help priests of integrity?

Then Father Walter raised his finger to the ceiling and said, "First, you have to find them. Just because a priest has not molested someone doesn't make him a priest of integrity. We cannot know from external appearance, or even behavior, what a priest of integrity is. Nor should we just divide priests into two groups: those who have abused children sexually, and those who did not. This lionizes those who have not earned it. The priest does not deserve to be lionized simply for not molesting, nor simply for speaking out, nor for supporting organizations like Voice of the Faithful. He shouldn't be awarded for any of it, that's just his job!

"Second," he added a finger, "you must call on your priest to be a priest of integrity by requiring it of him. Don't let a priest get away with an unprepared homily, or a ministry not supported by personal prayer. Don't let him live, act and speak as a prince when he should be a shepherd. Call us priests to task. Call us priests to be what we say we are for you."

"Third," the ring finger joined, "do what you're doing tonight. Gather together to pray, to listen, and to work.

"Fourth," the pinky arrived, "throw yourself into the life of your social parish community as you never have before. Every Sunday, the bulletin is full of events that offer opportunities to become active. Just as the faithful's voice needs to be heard here at this type of meeting, it should also be heard in other aspects of parish life. You have chosen to make this meeting a priority so, I ask you, how can we make the life of the church a priority?

"Finally," the whole palm open, all fingers to the sky, "don't let this die! Don't blink first. We are newcomers to what we are trying to do here. We are staring down professionals.

"The media have played a large role in bringing these issues to the surface for us, but beware! You are messing with an institution that wants this to go away, to silence you. The objective here is the union of voices."

He then sat down, but the outline of his palm remained like a ghostly imprint in the air.

It was this union of voices that seemed to be disturbing the church the most. As long as the laity remained disorganized and dormant, the hierarchy had no problem with them, but once they organized into a common voice in an attempt to help, the hierarchy did everything it could to disband them. But what were they afraid of? What other secrets were they keeping?

The fund to augment the ailing Cardinal's Appeal was brought up after Father Walter sat down. "I'm getting feedback from the Chancery that the fund is not a good idea, every agency will refuse it," said David, VOTF's financial advisor.

Steve Krueger then chimed in, "Rome may have their hands in this. I would not be surprised if they do."

Jim Post then pointed out that "It's a policy structure!"

Steve followed with, "It's in ignorance on how we intend the fund to work! It's a donor designated fund, not a Catholic charity."

Scott agreed, saying, "This is very important to communicate with precision."

David then brought it home, "Rome may be involved! No bishop wants to see his authority challenged!"

My thought was that the fund was a good thing. If people didn't want to give to the Cardinal's Appeal because they were angry with Cardinal Law, yet still wanted to help those in need, then the fund made perfect sense as a channel for that. However, the archdiocese appeared not to care so much about the needy. It appeared to only care about the prestige associated with distributing the funds. It did not want to share the limelight. This was underscored in an e-mail that was forwarded to me by a friend:

Dearest Friends,

It is with great sadness that I read of the bishops' latest power ploy. Can it be true that they really would deprive the poor and the needy of the archdiocese by refusing to accept funds that were offered for Catholic charities? What is the justification for denying help to the needy? It seems to me that their lust for power over the purse has deprived them of compassion. Do you remember my telling you that we were told that if the Cardinals Appeal is a failure, then the needy "will just have to go without?" I am concerned about allowing Bishop Edyvean to define the agenda for this upcoming meeting. And I question whether VOTF needs to spend time describing the process and particulars of the fund. You have already provided us with an intelligible contract. Let the bishop and the cardinal read it. I fear that this is a tactic to deflect attention away from the crucial and immediate need for the hierarchy to accept responsibility for their deplorable behavior.

The other issue brought up during the meeting was that the archdiocese was forbidding a Mass to take place at the Hynes Center during the convention. Since it was not taking place inside a church, it could not, and would not, be approved.

"Was the World Trade Center Mass approved?" Peggy asked.

"The Priest Forum thinks that we will get in trouble, they said not to have a mass—that we'll be playing right into their hands if we do!" Jim Post said.

Peggy came back with, "We meet the guidelines!"

"Vatican II says that we can do this," said Scott.

"This is about power and not about a Mass!" Peggy concluded.

"Why in the hell can't we say Mass at the Hynes Convention Center?" I asked myself.

Then Mary Ann Keyes stood. She was a petite, feisty, middle-aged Irish woman with a brogue one generation removed. She could comfort you in one moment then rip your head off the next. She was well connected to several bishops, and deeply informed on Catholic politics. She said, "I feel that we would benefit from the wisdom of a canon lawyer. Many decisions made by our bishops and cardinals have not followed canonical procedures, and if need be, we, the laity, have every right to appeal our case to the *Signatura*. We cannot be silenced! We are clearly within our rights to hold Mass.

21. IN THE CHAMBERS

Late that July, VOTF had a meeting with Bishop Edyvean. Before the meeting, I pushed VOTF to produce a joint news release. But, the matter of issuing a joint release became an internal battle. Tempers flared, conversations went back and forth. So, I called James Muller.

We sat down for coffee. James began speaking as he poured his cream: "Regarding not doing a joint press release, I find it entirely out of touch with what was decided at the steering committee meeting, what we told the press, and what is needed. I will send the press release to you with edits from Mary and Steve, who also like it. There is an entire specialty of issuing releases in conjunction with negotiations. I have done it many times and think we have much to gain from a joint message."

"I can't agree more," I said. "I'm not sure where this press release breakdown is occurring. Your experience is priceless. We both know the press moves on, stories grow cold, and the laity will settle back into the pews. At this point, VOTF hype and membership will plateau, if not drop off completely. To help keep the movement alive, we need to fall back on the 'good' press relations established in the first six months. In this manner, although we are pitching an old story, they will listen to fresh news, and move forward on it."

Once the meeting was adjourned, my job was to get the message approved through Donna Morrissey, Cardinal Law's spokesperson, and then out to the press; but when I tried to reach Ms. Morrissey, she was not available. I left message after message and got no return call. The Associated Press was asking for my comments, but I couldn't issue any because I didn't have approval—then the story hit the wires:

> Friday, a group of Catholics met with archdiocese officials to discuss creating a fund that would bypass the church hierarchy and give directly to church charities. The group, Voice of the Faithful, met Friday for the second time with Bishop Walter Edyvean, Cardinal Bernard Law's top administrator.
>
> Group spokesman Mike Emerton refused to comment on specifics. And archdiocese spokesman also would not comment Friday.
>
> The meeting came a day after the archdiocese announced it was slashing its budget for the coming fiscal year by $8 million, or one-third. The

archdiocese cited a weak economy for the cuts, which will affect aid to parishes, schools and hospitals.

I hated rendering a "no comment." My hope was that we really would get some substance, and have movement on the issues with a joint statement. I should have realized that Donna Morrissey was stonewalling. She played it well. She knew that we would not issue a statement unless it was approved. By stalling, the press would move on to file their stories. I was impressed, but I felt that I let VOTF down. I had one job to do, and I failed it. I let Donna Morrissey get the better of me. I vowed to not let that happen again. I decided that for future meetings with the bishop, our press conferences were going to be held in front of Cardinal Law's administrative office—without asking for approval. That, I figured, might entice Donna Morrissey to come to out to the microphones for a "joint" comment.

22. TO THE CENTER

There was no time for rest as I got ready for the convention at the Hynes Center. This event would attempt to accomplish in one day what the Catholic Church was unwilling to do for the several decades: gather victims of clergy sexual abuse, priests, theologians, scholars and concerned Catholics, and have an open discussion about the church's pedophile problem. This was an opportunity for the laity to learn about its sanctioned role within the church, from church historians and theologians, and in addition, VOTF wanted to put compassion into action by supporting and standing in solidarity with victims.

The messages needed to be tighter than the messages delivered in Dallas. The media was fully aware that the bishops were treating the laity harshly, and the press wanted to know what the laity was going to do about it. Three simple messages were delivered: First, the Laity are taking their church back via a larger role, which is within canon law and Vatican II; Second, the Laity are demanding accountability and that action be taken by bishops (true bishop accountability, not self-appointed review boards); Finally, VOTF affirms the teaching of Jesus and the fundamental beliefs of Catholicism.

As supported by the Bible, Canon Law, and Vatican II, the laity had the right and obligation to build up the body of Christ in each of us and in each of our parishes. Many rights granted to the laity by Vatican II had not been exercised. So, in response, VOTF envisioned a spiritual event, with open and honest communication, but most importantly, an event that would promote healing—something the Catholic Church couldn't accomplish with lawyers and money.

Because the Boston Archdiocese saw the event as troublesome, they issued an order strictly forbidding VOTF from having mass.

Anthony, a professor of Theology at a University in Philadelphia, came with a strategy. "First of all," he said, "let's make sure we have the official truth about what Law is up to. Try to get his reasons for the prohibition. I'm not a canon lawyer, but I don't believe that VOTF can say it has a right to a Mass at its meeting. If this is true, then VOTF should make a public announcement that you're profoundly sorry that Law will not permit forty-two hundred Catholics to have the Eucharist, when they are meeting in full compliance with Church teaching to help the Church, when it is actually the hierarchy that is the one in need of healing, and who, more than ever, need the Eucharist as the sign of unity and love that it is."

That was exactly the kind of information I needed to demonstrate how out of touch Cardinal Law really was with the laity, and to show that very little healing would be accomplished while he was in office.

But then Anthony admonished, "In no way should VOTF even hint, or deny, that Law is in charge and that he has the right to prohibit the mass. You should avoid all dissent and confrontation."

I knew it was critical to portray VOTF members as cool-headed centrists seeking cooperation. That way, it would be difficult for the archdiocese to label us as "dissidents." The bishops were deriding VOTF in the press. The *Boston Globe* reported Mexico's Archbishop, Cardinal Norberto Rivera, as calling the coverage of sex abuse scandals "a campaign of media persecution against the entire Catholic Church."

"Well," I thought, "How about that!"

After statements like that hit the wires, my cell phone would not stop ringing. I responded by saying that it was not the media that made this happen, and that the tree was rotten on the inside. This problem was a cancer that had to be rooted out but, in diocese after diocese across the country, we saw bishops trying to hide it, instead of tackling the problem head on, try to hide it. Comments like the cardinal's "media persecution" were part of some sort of counter offensive. If anything, the media needed to be thanked and applauded for the disclosure. If it weren't for the Globe's Spotlight Team, the world might never have known about the procedures that allowed child molesters and rapists to be shuffled from one parish to the next, nor would it have become aware of just how many victims there were. These were horrifying, appalling, numbers. The bishops were out of touch, the media was to be awarded, and it was now left up to the laity to force corrections.

The time for the convention was approaching. The permit to speak outside Faneuil Hall was granted. James Muller was going to deliver a speech at a podium in front of Faneuil Hall. It was my job to make sure the press was there and that a crowd was assembled. As noon approached, I started to relax as all the press one could want, and a crowd bigger than could be expected had gathered. It was perfect, except for one little thing that needed attention. James Muller wasn't there. *Where's James?* Then my phone rang. It was James. He said that he was stuck in traffic and that I would have to deliver his speech. My mouth went dry, and my hands trembled. The sun rose high above Faneuil

Hall, and it grew hot. I sat down on the stone steps to study his speech. I read it as fast as I could over and over. I knew it well, too, for I read it many times the night before, but I just wasn't comfortable with this idea of me delivering it. I couldn't help wondering what my work colleagues and friends and family would see on the local news, and I couldn't stop thinking about the questions they might ask. I looked up at the broadcast trucks. The lights shined. It was time! Hundreds had gathered in front of the podium. The grandeur, sanctity, and importance of Faneuil Hall stood in the background. I clutched a water bottle, stepped to the podium, adjusted the microphone and began to speak:

> Good afternoon, I am Michael Emerton, Media Director of Voice of the Faithful. We are a grassroots organization of over 20,000 lay Catholics formed in response to the clergy sexual abuse crisis.
>
> This press conference of Voice of the Faithful is held in this historic location for a special reason. Over 200 years ago Samuel Adams and other citizens of Boston met here to debate the response to injustices perpetrated by those with absolute power. Today the survivors of sexual abuse by those exercising such power in the Catholic Church step forward to express their freedom and ensure that such abuse will not be forced on subsequent generations.
>
> The Voice of the Faithful asserts, in this cradle of liberty, that a representative democratic process for the laity, using many of the principles developed here 200 years ago, will be added to the structure of the Catholic Church.
>
> Out of Boston, a response to the underlying problem of abuse of absolute power has arisen as it did in 1776. The parallels suggest the work of the Holy Spirit. A city that gave democracy as a remedy for a secular autocratic rule in the 18th century now offers a democratic process for the Catholic laity suffering under a medieval, autocratic structure in the 21st century. Voice of the Faithful brings a structure to prevent abuses that inevitably arise from the existence of absolute power, a structure that can be used, in the spirit of Vatican II, to complement the role of the hierarchy in proclaiming the undisputed revelations of Jesus Christ, and build, from the ashes left by the conflagration, a better church.

I then introduced Paul:

> As Mike has noted, we are here at Faneuil Hall for one reason. This is

hallowed ground in the history of our country, and the place where voices have been raised for over two and a half centuries in the search for justice and liberty. In Rome, the pope spoke. In Dallas, the bishops spoke. Now, in Boston, the mainstream Catholic laity speaks. We respond in a spirit of hope that the leadership of our beloved church will be accountable to the people they govern, and that the people they govern will exercise their right to participate responsibly in policy and administration.

All of us must be accountable to speak openly and transparently about the issues raised by the sexual abuse scandal. If healing and reconciliation are to be achieved, then we need to cleanse the deep wound of hurt by speaking truth to power on these matters, even if it is painful. Only then will trust be restored.

We call on the bishops to work honestly and proactively with civil authorities, using both civil and canonical procedures to close loopholes and tighten the system to protect children. Canon law alone has not been sufficient in the past to assure protection. Where revisions are needed to implement the bishops' new policy, they must be sought. Provisions in civil and criminal law such as the statute of limitations, release of all documents on abusive priests, mandatory reporting by all clergy, any contributory negligence clauses that apportion blame to parents and victims are all issues that Voice of the Faithful is studying carefully.

Paul then introduced Mary:

Let me review what Voice of the Faithful is doing to move beyond words and get down to work: Five initiatives are being pursued: the development of Parish Voice chapters across the nation and abroad (for example, inquiries have already been received from Germany, Scotland, and Japan); a database of priests involved in abuse to help survivors learn about their molesters and make contact with other victims; a bishop monitoring form to follow compliance by our local bishops with the norms adopted in Dallas; fundraising for survivor advocacy groups; and establishment of a Voice of Compassion Fund to allot contributions to agencies and services affected by cutbacks. We are accountable for our actions just as the bishops are for theirs.

Our congress at the Hynes Convention Center tomorrow will close with a Mass and Eucharist, calling thousands of Catholics across the spectrum of opinion, to pray together for healing, reconciliation and the restoration of trust in our church leadership.

The bishops have an exemplary record of reaching out to the marginalized in our society: the poor, the sick, the immigrant, the vulnerable, and the aged. We call on the bishops to reach out to those who feel marginalized within their own church—the laity, devoted men and women whose hearts yearn for true healing made visible in action and deed. We urge the bishops to trust that we, too, want to build a prayerful, loving church for the future. Today, tomorrow, and henceforth, hear our voice, the Voice of the Faithful.

The event went well. We built attention and received additional coverage right before our big convention.

23. THE CONVENTION

Later that night, I sat down in my living room to assemble 500 press kits. I had all the documents in neat piles, stretching from one end of the room to the other. The process was simple, pick one copy of each document from the first row, and place it in the left hand side of the press kit folder, then pick up one document from each pile in the second row, and place it in the right hand side of the press kit folder. It took awhile.

One of the documents was a petition written by theologians that outlined VOTF's right to exist. Many bishops were asserting that the group had no right to exist and that it was a dangerous group composed of dissidents. So to combat this, VOTF asked a group of theologians to document the reasons why the group should exist. The document read (in part) as follows:

> As Theologians, we support the rights and responsibilities of lay Catholics, acting in the grace of their spiritual gifts, to gather in the spirit of Christ, who dwells within the whole church… These rights and responsibilities of lay Catholics are part of the official Catholic teaching, and we encourage all Catholics to read the documents of Vatican II… Thus, we fully support the right and responsibility of Voice of the Faithful to meet in prayerful discernment of the signs of the times and to present to the hierarchy for the confirmation and implementation, what their sense of faith requires them to voice.

The signatures of seventy seventy-one prominent theologians from such places as Yale University Divinity School, Boston College, College of the Holy Cross, Emory University, Loyola University, Harvard Divinity School, Marquette University, Georgetown University, University of San Francisco, Villanova University, Temple University, and St. Jerome's University in Ontario, Canada, were appended.

Earlier that day, James Muller had given press interview about the convention. So, after stuffing the folders, I turned on the TV, and I watched James deliver the new messages perfectly.

The morning of the convention, I arrived in Boston early with my mother, Valerie. She wanted to help with the press table and hand out press kits. We carried boxes from the parking lot to the center. As we approached, I noticed that protesters had gathered.

A man in a green shirt, blue shorts, and a Michigan State hat was yelling into a bullhorn, "Raped! Molested! Dead!" Another man, standing next to him, carried a sign that said: Stop Look and Listen. He looked to be about 30 years old and wore a white T-shirt and green shorts. I then noticed an overweight man, possibly in his 30s, wearing black shorts and a purple shirt holding up a sign that simply said: Lock-Up Law! And they were handing out their own literature. I took a flyer, and I read it.

REJECT CARDINAL LAW:

Reject the leadership of Cardinal Law! Let every good Catholic support a moratorium on attendance at services in all parishes of the Boston archdiocese on Sunday, September 22. Do not continue to bring shame on the Catholic religion by accepting the leadership of a man who knowingly allowed hundreds of our children to be raped and molested month after month, year after year, decade after decade. Bernard Law's actions are not those of a Christian; he is not a Christian; he is a cardinal in and leader in name only, not in fact. Show him this on September 22.

I grabbed several more flyers. I figured it would be best to keep track of the radical voices. Once inside, I took a stroll around the convention center to see how the event was being put together. I took the escalator to the second floor. As I came off the escalator on the second floor, I noticed two hallways leading into the auditorium. One was lined with giant poster boards that were covered with handwritten letters, poems and pictures donated by survivors. It was the Hall of Survivors. Several people were tacking up letters. I walked up to the first board and began reading. My eyes began to tear up. I pulled away. *You've got to stay focused. You've got to concentrate. Toughen-up little man or we'll never get through this.*

The other hallway was lined with eight-foot-long folding tables. People were unpacking boxes on them, pulling out books, setting up videos, and hanging crosses to sell. I decided to head down that hall on my way to the auditorium. I couldn't bring myself to walk past those letters.

I entered the auditorium through a large set of double doors to check in on the audio and video. The entire scene reminded me of roadies getting ready for a concert, as people adjusted lights, rolled out cords, banged on microphones, and climbed scaffolding. It was inspirational to think that just five months ago this whole thing started because several concerned Catholics stayed after Mass one day to have a discussion, and now the world was in on it. I looked up at a huge video screen just as it turned on. At the podium, a technician checked the sound. His image was broadcast to empty seats. A layer of goose bumps ran from the back of my arms to the base of my neck. I knew something special was happening.

I left the auditorium energized. If we pulled this off, I knew we would have the leverage needed to truly make a change within the Church and help rid this cancer that had been eating away its core. I headed to room 107—the press room. It was a quiet place to get away from the noise, with plenty of outlets and phone ports. I realized the importance of having a separate pressroom when I worked with the Commission on Presidential Debates. I took a glance at the press list in my pocket and saw that over a hundred media organizations had registered. It was going to be a busy day. I then looked over the agenda of speakers and scanned the breakout sessions. The passion of the people was reflected in the topics. I wanted to go to so many of them, but I knew I couldn't--they were talking about things that were too close to me; I would be an emotional wreck. I needed to focus on setting up meetings, verifying facts, and assuring messages were on point.

I put the agenda aside, picked out Jim Post's letter from the press kit, and scanned it. Then I opened the declaration to Rome and looked at the news release, which read in part:

> In a unanimous vote tallied at one of the largest gatherings of Catholic laity in recent years, Voice of the Faithful, a grassroots organization of over 19,000 lay Catholics, proclaim their right to actively call for Church renewal. The declaration read (in part)... We the faithful, in order to form a more perfect Church, gather in Boston on this 20th day of July 2002, to affirm the role of the laity in the constant renewal of the Catholic Church, as proclaimed in Lumen Gentium and other documents of the Second Vatican Council. We acknowledge with grief and anger the profound suffering of untold numbers of boys and girls, men and women, sexually abused by our clergy. We honor those heroic survivors who have come forward to tell their terrible truth. We dedicate our apostolate to building up a church in which these crimes and the abuse of power that made them possible, will not happen again.

I had a list of all VOTF's chapters currently in operation. There were more than 100, mostly in Massachusetts, with many others starting weekly in other states including Connecticut, New York, Minnesota, Oklahoma, Pennsylvania, Wisconsin, and Iowa. I also had a list of convention attendees, who hailed from all 50 states.

As the morning progressed, people started filing in. There was a sense of jubilation as they filled the main hall. Eventually the floor space filled, followed by the orchestra, and then the balconies. As the auditorium lights dimmed, the crowd settled in.

James Muller opened,

"Good morning, my name is James Muller. And I cannot believe what I'm looking at!"

The crowd erupted in applause. It took several minutes for it to die down. Then he continued,

How can we overcome the dilemma of consciousness that many of us feel, our anger is justified, but we recognize our responsibility to our neighbors in need. The answer in part is to create new ways of doing things. Voice of the Faithful is developing new tools for a new era of Catholicism. The causation of the terrible problems of clergy sexual abuse, and institutional cover-up, can be viewed as the analysis of causation of death that is written on a death certificate. The certificate starts with the visual problem, a death, and then identifies the approximate causes such as a heart attack, and the underlying cause such as atherosclerosis. The death, in this case, is the tragedy of the dual problems of clergy sexual abuse and the cover-up. Many share an appreciation of the underlying cause as the existence of centralized power that is neither checked, nor balanced. Voice of the Faithful is concerned with the underlying cause of the problem.

We need to shift the balance of leadership back in our direction to make our own lay leadership more conclusive of the real spectrum of diversity in the Catholic Church. I'm convinced that the VOTF is a movement of God's Holy Spirit in our time and place. This is not to canonize everything that they will do over the next 200 years. This critical time, at this historic gathering, we would do well to heed the words of the letter to James, 'Anyone who listens to the word but does not do what it says is like a man who looks at his face in a mirror and, after looking at himself, goes away and immediately forgets what he looks like.' We must listen with care. We must speak truth. We must act with faith, love and courage. And we must act now! There is nothing hidden that will not be revealed.

I bounced back and forth from the pressroom to the auditorium all afternoon. NPR wanted James Muller for immediate comment; Channel 5 was looking to set up a live interview; Reuters wanted to speak with survivors; and WNYC wanted to set up a meet and greet of New York folks in the press room.

When I wasn't bouncing, I was crouching below the stage, a small figure taking notes, or I was a marginal figure standing off-camera, making sure our spokespeople stayed on message. At the end of the day, much to the annoyance of the Boston Archdiocese, a Mass was held. A procession entered the auditorium. A small boy dressed in white carried a simple wooden cross, followed by a boy and a girl carrying tall white candles in golden holders. Red roses led the way for the Holy Bible, which was held up by Luise Cahill Dittrich. Several banners with the word "Peace" flanked by pictures of white doves flowed behind her.

Susan took the stage and spoke, "Jesus Christ gathers us together as a sign of unity and strength. A great meal of Thanksgiving for all the blessings and gifts that each of us shares…" Reverend William then said the mass, wearing green, and standing next to a seven seven-foot cross draped with purple and red ribbons. "We offer our Mass this evening in a special way, for those who are survivors of abuse. We offer our Mass for their families. We offer this Mass for their healing."

As I listened, memories kept pushing-up tears, so I escaped to the press room. Several journalists were writing stories, and photographers were sending photos via the phone ports. I took a seat in the back and then opened my notebook. I just sat there staring at the page in a trance, not reading anything, when an old craggy voice from behind snapped me out of it, "What do you think of all this?"

Startled, I turned around to see a gray-haired man handwriting his story on several pieces of loose paper. "It's certainly a big event, and one that was definitely needed," I said to him.

"Are you a Catholic?" He asked me.

"Yes, I grew up Catholic and went to church in a city about an hour north of Boston.

He then asked me about Cardinal Law and registered some derogatory comments about bishops in general. I told him that I agreed with him and that there were several high-ranking individuals that should be in prison.

He then smiled at me and said, "You're a good young Catholic. Stay that way." He then gathered up his notes, picked up his cell phone, and began dictating his story. *Man, this guy is old school!* After he stood up, he put his hand on my shoulder and said, "Take care."

Two journalists sitting several rows away immediately came over. One of them said, "Do you know who you were just talking to?"

Looking up, I said, "No. But he seemed like a nice guy."

The journalists then looked at me dumbfounded and said, "That was Jimmy Breslin—he's not known for being congenial!"

At the time, I didn't know who Jimmy Breslin was, so I said, "Well, he seems to be in a pretty good mood, today."

24. FEET TO THE FIRE

The Boston convention and the Dallas Bishops Conference put The Archdiocese of Boston where I wanted them—on the defensive, getting hotheaded, and making mistakes.

The *New York Times* ran a story on VOTF's Boston convention with the following information: "In a response to a type of report card VOTF issued to its members in order to track their perspective bishop's compliance with the Dallas Charter, Mike Emerton was quoted as saying, 'This will hold the bishops' feet to the fire in terms of Dallas.'"

I thought the Bishops Report Card would be one of our more powerful tools, but that was nothing in comparison to the Voice of Compassion Fund. Just a day after our convention, Donna Morrissey issued a statement on behalf of Cardinal Law which read (in part), "As has been communicated in the media, Voice of the Faithful has announced an initiative whereby it will collect and find ways to distribute funds from persons who choose at this time not to contribute to the Cardinal's Appeal. The Archdiocese cannot accept the monies collected in this manner. This approach of donating money does not recognize the role of the Archbishop.

The *Globe* ran an article, written by Sacha Pfeiffer, with the headline, "Law to Reject Donations from Voice of the Faithful." I could not have asked for any better press. For the first time, Cardinal Law was responding directly to VOTF. He specifically stated that he would not accept any funds that VOTF raised to help hospitals, schools or ministries. This was a shocking revelation, as the Cardinal's Appeal was significantly down, $4.8 million, compared with the $7.5 million it had gathered at the same time the year before. Boston Catholics were upset with Cardinal Law, and he was refusing to take money to increase his fund.

The *Globe* had an archdiocesan spokesman on record as saying that Voice of the Faithful's initiative, "Does not recognize the role of The Archbishop and his responsibility in providing for the various programs and activities of the church. Any money donated to those agencies by Voice of the Faithful would have to be routed through the archdiocese, which would refuse to accept the funds."

The Boston Archdiocese simply refused to change its attitude and was, as usual, protecting its reputation, first and foremost, at the expense of anybody, or anything. Statements like these were exactly what I needed in order to demonstrate that it was a regime change that would start the healing.

I placed a quote from Jim Post with the press: "The Cardinal's Appeal failed on its own, and it failed because of the reason we all know, the scandal in the church."

Jim's quote was buttressed with one from David Clohessy, national director of the Survivor's Network of those Abused by Priests (SNAP): "I never thought I would see the day when any Catholic official advocated any roadblock in helping the poor. The mission of the church is to help the needy in every way possible, regardless of whose return address is on the check."

We called a meeting to talk about possible responses to these quotes. Jim Post said, "The morning headlines say it clearly: the archdiocese has declared war on the Voice of Compassion Fund. When he became prime minister at the outset of World War II, Churchill was asked to describe his program. His response then, and ours today, is terse and to the point: 'Victory, Victory, Victory!'" He then outlined several talking points:

1. Voice is about building up, not tearing down the church.
2. Cutbacks and closing all programs damage the church.
3. Voice of Compassion is designed to alleviate pain, help people, etc.
4. Roman Catholic Archdiocese of Boston (RCAB) clearly does not understand what the Voice of Compassion fund is about.
5. This is because they refused to meet with us.
6. We remain ready to meet with Cardinal Law.

David registered his comments. "I think that we should have not only a press release but also a press conference this afternoon to respond to the archdiocese's press release. I think Jim Post should be our spokesman, because he has an excellent manner of balancing hot and cold while making points cogently and forcefully. He is a nice moderate voice."

Bill Cadigan added, "As one of those who attended the last meeting with Edyvean during which he promised us a meeting to discuss the Voice of Compassion Fund, I am particularly galled that the archdiocese has chosen to oppose our efforts without learning the facts. Anything I can do to help make our point of view known, let me know."

Terry urged us to put several issues up front: "We haven't ever advised people not to give to the Cardinal's Appeal; we have only said that if they feel they cannot do so in good conscience, that we are simply providing them with a way of continuing to support the poor and disadvantaged.

"By rejecting this offer, Cardinal Law is hurting the poor in order to hurt the laity and assert his position. This is a huge propaganda mistake for them, and we should capitalize on it."

Paul Baier characterized the archdiocese's response as a public challenge: "I truly believe that the message from Cardinal Law's spokesperson today is so clear and challenging, that we must respond. He told us what his priorities are, namely controlling us takes precedence over the needs of the poor. I do not have a specific suggestion, but I believe we need to respond to this public challenge; to fail to do so would be an enabling act."

We were also receiving hundreds of messages from chapter constituents such as this one from Westford, Massachusetts: "I was very disappointed to see that Cardinal Law has rejected VOTF's attempt to channel money to various charities. I am disappointed but not surprised. What surprises me is that VOTF tried to work with Cardinal Law. He will continue to stonewall laypeople until he either leaves or is forced to leave. Until then, there will be no change and any attempt to meet him halfway will end in disappointment. Be strong and stay the course. There are charities that will gladly accept the money. Our family has adopted a poor parish up in New Hampshire and also sends contributions directly to Catholic Charities. We are diverging from Cardinal Law and our local parish that still supports his every action. I pray each week that God will provide guidance to bring our church back to him and the people. It appears the journey will be longer than I expected."

I needed to use these stern voices to give an edgy response. By the end of the day, I had hit every Boston-based news source with our rebuttal, drawn from the suggestions of the group. I had someone talk to the *Boston Herald* about how the fund worked. As a result of that interview we learned that Catholic Charities and Caritas Christi had not been offered any funds yet, have had not turned any down, and would consult their boards of trustees before deciding their course.

I pointed another member to the local Boston news channels, someone who had a way of explaining the absurdity of the situation like a frustrated, concerned father.

I also needed a more reserved and tempered voice, one that was well grounded in the institutional matters of the church—it turned out that Steve

Krueger was perfect for this. I placed him with *The Emily Rooney Show*, which aired on WGBH.

I took on the Associated Press, *Wall Street Journal*, *New York Times* and *USA Today*. An excerpt from the Associated Press story entitled, "Boston Archdiocese Won't Accept Funds from Laity-led Reform Group," reported: "VOTF, a group born out of the Roman Catholic priest sex abuse scandal, has proposed creating a fund that would bypass the church hierarchy and give directly to archdiocese charities. 'The approach does not recognize the role of the archbishop and his responsibility in providing for the various programs and activities of the church,' Donna Morrissey, spokeswoman for Cardinal Bernard Law, said in a statement. Mike Emerton, a spokesman for VOTF said the group was 'a little confused' by the announcement because it had not fully explained the fund to the archdiocese. 'If the Cardinal's Appeal is down 30 to 40 percent, and programs have to be closed, and the public knows there's a pool of money waiting, that the laity contributed, to make sure that the organizations are running, and the Archdiocese flat-out refuses to accept it, that would be a very unfortunate situation,' Emerton said."

A *New York Times* article, "Archdiocese to Refuse Gifts That Thwart Bishop's Power," captured this: "Today, Michael Emerton, a VOTF spokesman, said that the group was not encouraging people to avoid giving to the archdiocese, but was simply providing an alternative for 'people who already made that conscious decision not to donate to the Cardinal's Appeal.'"

USA Today wrote: "VOTF, a lay group formed earlier this year, is gaining nonprofit status to raise money directly for Boston-area church ministries. 'The effort could serve as a blueprint for redirecting donations in other U.S. diocese' spokesman Mike Emerton says."

Several days later, the *Wall Street Journal* ran its story: "'Furthermore, VOTF has plans to turn itself into an institutional force contemplating a $1 million annual budget and a staff of 40 or 50,' according to spokesman, Mike Emerton.

After going through gantlets like this, I grew more comfortable speaking with the press, especially the Boston-based broadcast reporters, such as Kelley Tuthill from WCVB Channel 5. She was following the scandal very closely, and I often had extended discussions with her about VOTF's movement and the archdiocese's treatment of the laity.

In addition, the incorrect statement about Catholic Charities not accepting the funds took on a life of its own. The *Boston Globe* covered it in a story entitled, "In Rift with Law, Agency To Accept Lay Group's Funds." The article stated that in contradiction to Cardinal Law, Catholic Charities said that they would accept donations from VOTF, and they criticized Law for rejecting the group's fundraising plan. "We will not turn down any donation," declared the spokeswoman for Catholic Charities in the article.

The *Globe* quoted a Catholic Charities board member, "I was surprised because it was inconsistent with what we've been saying about accepting donations from people who perhaps are not comfortable giving to the Cardinal's Appeal.

Thomas P. O'Neill III, former lieutenant governor and a one-time adviser to Cardinal Law, characterized the Cardinal's decision as "another example of the archdiocese not listening and not understanding the flock.

Just two days after the incorrect comment, Boston Archdiocese officials retracted a portion of their statement, saying instead that Catholic Charities, Caritas Christi, and other church-affiliated organizations may choose to accept donations from VOTF.

Not only was VOTF showing that the Boston Archdiocese was putting its pride over the poor, but the group was also illustrating that archdiocese clearly did not have its facts straight.

As this dispute played out, several members of Boston's Priest Forum, who were bold enough to speak up, were beginning to feel pressure from the hierarchy. I received and e-mail from Father Bob: "Hey Mike, Congrats to you all on a great gathering Saturday. VOTF has done more to heal and strengthen our community than any other entity in the church. God is with you. I'm a little concerned about growing media attention on my parish and me, though. The *New York Times* sort of caught me off guard yesterday because I had not heard about the archdiocese's decision to reject the Voice of Compassion Funds. I continue to find myself a little alone in all this. I will continue to do all I can to support the efforts of VOTF, but in the same spirit of your organization, I do not want to appear too radical or isolated… I guess I am just asking for your advice regarding continued media attention and my concerns about acting alone. I welcome the chance to inspire dialog and have no problem speaking with the media. I believe The Spirit is leading. I just want to be of the best service to my church and VOTF. ~ Peace."

The article he was referring to was in the *New York Times*, entitled, "Archdiocese to Refuse Gifts That Thwart Bishop's Power." "Father Bob, Pastor of St. Catherine's, in a housing project in the Charlestown section of Boston, expressed a strong disappointment, 'I would challenge them to say how they are going to help the people here,' he said, referring to archdiocese officials. St. Catherine's would probably benefit from the fund. This year, Father Bob said, the archdiocese cut its annual contribution to his church from $70,000 to $50,000. The decision, Father Bob said, 'seems to say to me that the archdiocese doesn't yet understand the critical nature of the problem,' that 'because of their frustration, people are linking their feelings about the church to their donations.'" He then added, "I think it's going to heighten people's dismay with the operations of the church, heighten their frustrations and their calls for change when this door is being shut."

My heart went out to Father Bob, and the next day I drove to Charlestown to have a conversation with him. He was a joyful and compassionate man in charge of an inner city parish in the middle of a depressed neighborhood. We strolled around inside the church as he expanded upon how isolated and alone he and the other priests were feeling. He also spoke at great length about how the priests felt caught between their duty to the church and what they felt was truly right.

We then exited the church, and he showed me a dilapidated brick building located in the parking lot. "What's this place?" I asked.

"We started to refurbish this building into a youth center," he replied. "But we ran out of money."

I squeezed my way through a front door that was falling off its hinges and took a step in. As I looked around, I could see that the restoration had been abandoned. Empty paint cans and hardened paintbrushes were scattered about, bits of drywall were pulverized on the floor. Rooms in the back of the building contained broken furniture illuminated by streaks of sunlight coming through cracks in the plywood over the windows.

"It's got a lot of potential, but there's nothing we can do right now, so it just sits here," said Father Bob.

I took another minute and looked around the building. I imagined the good work that could be done in a place such as this. It surely would give the kids somewhere to go. I felt a fire in my belly, and my face hardened. I turned to Father Bob and said, "Let me paint a picture here for you.

"Cardinal Law, in his infinite wisdom, is going to refuse funds that VOTF has raised to help those in need. This is a perfect example of what those funds could be used for, but it lies in decay because of his arrogance. If the Archdiocese of Boston does not accept the fund, then we will find a way ourselves to fund projects like these with the monies donated."

"That would be great!" Father Bob said.

Then I put my hand on his shoulder and said, "If that happens, I need you to gather up all the children you work with, and have them stand in front of this building. I will then call every member of the press to come here as we announce that Cardinal Law has refused VOTF donations and that we are donating directly to refurbish this youth center."

25. DISSENSION

In addition to fighting for the fund, I had a couple of fires to put out regarding some members who spoke at the convention. *CRISIS Magazine* was coming down hard on VOTF. It was calling the group "wolves in sheep's clothing" as well as "dissidents." In August, *CRISIS* outlined its grievances in an editorial entitled, "Another Look at Voice of the Faithful." They claimed to have spoken to several people who attended VOTF meetings and who said that they were silenced and booed when they aired their traditional Catholic views. The editorial went on to say that traditional Catholics had asserted that VOTF should be charged with "distortion." Not stopping there, it then focused on some of the highly recommended reading materials listed on VOTF's website, including Anthony's guide to renewing and restructuring the church.

CRISIS was asserting that Anthony had an agenda and pointed to his views that the sexual abuse scandal evolved from the hierarchy's "ignorance of the human body and sex, a mindset that degrades women and marriage, and spiritually distorted, psychologically troubled view of celibacy."

For the first six months of VOTF's existence, the group played the role of good guy in the press. Now, VOTF was put into the position of having to defend itself against claims of hypocrisy. I began to wonder if we were losing key members of our support base because the messages weren't defined.

In an Associated Press article titled, 'Lay Catholics See Chance For Change Amid Sex Scandal,' the story said that some U.S. bishops were concerned about "effective consultation of the laity and the participation of God's people in the decision-making that affects their well-being." In this story, though, it seemed that *CRISIS* was on VOTF's side. A small paragraph said that the editor of *CRISIS* "thinks bishops should concentrate on doctoring, education and worship, and welcome lay advice on professional and administrative matters."

A quote in the article from a VOTF member said it was time to end "Couch Potato Catholicism," and she described how VOTF was formed, "when we understood how many children were hurt."

Jim Post, in an e-mail to one of our members, explained VOTF's position:

> It appears that a number of dogs have been encouraged to attack us, especially on the issue of the 'voices' that spoke at the July 20th convention. Our position has been that the Catholic laity is entitled and needs to hear from individuals who have studied the issues, work in

professional fields, and struggled to sort out the cross currents of research and scholarship…we sought to present a variety of views and an overall balance of positions. VOTF did not endorse the specific comments of any speaker but sought to create a forum for discussion and thought. Individuals can, and should, legitimately challenge any speaker's point of view. They should also raise questions about the sources and veracity of opinions. This is the essence of free speech and it is how we become an informed laity. ~ Best Wishes, Jim Post.

Terry was also lending a hand with damage control, and read this e-mail from a VOTF group member:

Have we learned our lesson yet? We're being tricked into giving responses that the press can twist. Let's get back to what we do best— Keep the faith, change the church! The CRISIS article forces us to think about what issues we presume to care about. We've been warned about our emphasis of Anthony's article before—it's a good one, but calling it highly recommended indicates that we endorse it. In fact, we haven't endorsed the idea of a constitution including the laity, which is the centerpiece of what Anthony wants to do. Anthony makes traditionalists who are on the fence nervous. We should put Anthony and lots of other stuff, including traditionalist approaches, in a 'voices on structural change' section. Traditionalists worry that we are a stalking horse for excerpts with agendas. And we need to remember that this crisis has hit traditional Catholics very hard, even harder than it has hit me and you and other progressive Catholics. It's very difficult for traditional Catholics to admit that some bishops were culpable and that the pope hasn't done enough. But we all agree for the most part about the crisis itself. The solution is to concentrate on the crisis and to search together for common ground on goals and solutions. Otherwise, we will squander a huge opportunity to make good come out in the crisis. We can't do good if we are just 35,000 mostly progressive Catholics.

Internal Catholicism questions were now being publicly raised. What does it mean to be Catholic? Can you believe in woman priests, but not abortion? Also, a negative sentiment toward VOTF was in the press. Requests to be removed from the e-mail list came flooding in, "Please remove my name from your e-mail/membership list. Though I have basically supported your mission, I heard on the radio that one of your speakers at the meeting in Boston was affiliated with Planned Parenthood. Mr. Emerton's explanation of why this person was chosen to speak doesn't answer the question as to why she was a featured part of the program. I do feel that the laity needs a stronger voice, and the present crisis is devastating. However, I am concerned that VOTF may have an agenda down the road that I do not agree with. I'm a 53-year-old, lifelong Catholic, CCD teacher for many years, a parochial school parent, etc. I was thrilled to see VOTF emerge, hoping that it would guide the Church back to its true mission and the basic principles. Unfortunately, I do not see Planned Parenthood's values as part of that mission. If my concerns are unfounded, please accept my apologies. However, I need to remove my name from your membership list at this time."

Paul responded to as many e-mails as possible, such as this one: "I'm an active lifetime Catholic, shamed and shocked by the sex scandals and the Chancery culture that encouraged the recycling of offenders, the bullying of victims, the payoffs and cover-ups. I am considering starting a parish Voice chapter at St. Mary's, but I have a problem and hope you can help me get some answers. I heard from another parishioner that an officer of SEICUS (Sex Education and Inform Counsel of the US) was an invited speaker for the national VOTF group. This is disturbing because this person holds that it is not necessarily morally objectionable for an adult man or woman to seek sexual gratification with a minor, and that, on the contrary, it can be helpful and meaningful. If this person still believes these views, it is as clear as daylight that she is part of the problem, not part of the solution.

Paul responded: "In terms of the person who spoke at our meeting, we were unaware of her background. We pulled together the speakers in four weeks, and she was highly recommended to us. VOTF does not stand for any teachings currently outside the official church positions (e.g., Pro-choice), but we believe very strongly that Catholics and VOTF need to be tolerant and inclusive (i.e., listen and understand opposing points of view) of many of these controversial issues (gays, married priests, clericalism, etc.). To be clear, this person you refer to was invited by VOTF and she spoke, but she does not represent any view of VOTF."

In the end, it was decided that we should distance ourselves from the woman affiliated with Planned Parenthood, as well as the one with past ties to SEICUS, and to put out a disclaimer on Anthony's guide. The anti-VOTF groups had a field day with this. They all pointed out that VOTF was disjointed and in a cover-up of their own.

I believed it was right to include all voices in the Catholic spectrum and to make sure that the general population had access to materials that would help them make informed decisions about their faith.

Anthony expressed his concerns with our response to his article. He wrote in an e-mail, "I've just seen the new website and the disclaimer over my guide. Since my guide first appeared on the old website, I have been sent e-mails from all over the world from people who received it well, learned from it, and took encouragement from it. Many came from lapsed and disgusted Catholics who read the Guide and joined VOTF. The disclaimer may very well now confuse these people or even hurt them. I will not allow anyone to be hurt in my name. Either remove the disclaimer or take my Guide off the website. Whichever you do, do it now! ~ Tony."

Damage control tactics were overlooked, and the group now had a black eye. I was disgusted with myself for not preparing VOTF for this and wondered if I should resign. *I'm not the one to lead this group's communications. I don't have what it takes to guide them through these turbulent waters. They need someone better. They need someone with more experience, someone who has enough foresight to head off potential damage. I'm not that person! They are not a group of seasoned politicians; they are ordinary people. They are a group of lay Catholics trying to address the sexual abuse problems within the church, and I'm a PR hack from the tech world exorcising his demons. Any more damaging situations like these—this group is finished, and it will be my fault.*

26. BANNED

The pressure was unbearable, but somehow, in some manner, I found the strength to continue. Something pushed me to get out of bed and work this to a conclusion. I wanted my old life back, but I couldn't stop what I was being led to do. To add to my worries, dioceses across the country were now banning VOTF chapters from their churches. E-mails began to pour in from all over the country, like this one from Philadelphia:

> Dear faithful people, I am a committee member of the Synod of Laity in Bishop Gregory's Belleville Dioceses. We are trying to communicate with him, and he has ignored us very well. We are planning a second Synod in September, and he has put fear in every church in the area because of the controversy. He finally answered our letters avoiding the concerns we have and said we should read Lumen Gentium. I wonder if you could explain what this is? Keep up the good work.

In the Bridgeport, Connecticut diocese, after Bishop Lori barred VOTF from meeting on church property, our Norwalk chapter began meeting at a local Congregational Church. The *Hartford Courant* quoted Bishop Lori as saying that our agenda is in conflict with the teachings of the Catholic faith. My rebuttal was, "The problem is a lack of understanding of what the Voice of the Faithful fund is. Those who have met with us have come away with different impressions.

In Newark, New Jersey, Archbishop Myers barred us from meeting on church property. Archbishop Myers also went so far as to chastise us, calling us "anti-church and anti-catholic," as well as saying that we "act as a cover for dissidents."

In Camden, Bishop Nicholas joined Archbishop Myers in banning VOTF from church property. Among the bans, one of the most publicly covered was the Diocese of Rockville Centre, New York. We had a very smart and active group in Rockville Centre that was backed by members of the clergy, as illustrated by this message:

> I have been a priest for over 56 years, and I have never felt so disappointed in our bishops as I am today for their antagonistic stance against VOTF. I went to Boston for the VOTF convention, and I was deeply impressed by the sincere love and loyalty for the Catholic faith. While some

members believe that there shouldn't be mandatory celibacy for priests, nor should there be bans on contraception, the VOTF leadership was careful not to call for any changes except for greater collegiality and accountability on the part of the hierarchy, as already called for by Vatican II. Then, when I read that some bishops refused to allow these dedicated people to meet in church buildings that they, themselves, had paid for, I was profoundly ashamed.

It was good to know that we had allies; people understood the fact that the laity's money had paid for these church facilities and that bishops were blocking their use. This became apparent to me after a television interview for a local Boston news station. During the interview, I spoke about a letter from Bishop Allue that implied that VOTF would cause a scandal if it established a chapter at Saint Michael's in North Andover, Massachusetts. Sitting on a park bench in the town common of North Andover, I explained to the reporter that we were "striving to open dialog and prevent misunderstandings." I really wanted to say that most bishops were pigheaded and would rather talk down to people from their pulpits than sit across from them and have a conversation.

When the camera was turned off, the reporter said to me that she could not understand why people were being banned from their own churches. She then opened her notebook, wrote down a number, and handed it to me, saying, "Call this person if you need a place to meet in this area, they will offer you facilities free of charge." I graciously accepted and forwarded the number to our North Andover leader.

The North Andover banning became such a big issue that we decided to put out a press release. The release stated that we expressed "deep disappointment" to learn that the bishop has banned its members from assembling on parish property. I quoted a person from the parish who said, "We love our church dearly, and all we have sought from the beginning was an open and honest dialog with our bishops. This crisis in our beloved church was not of our making. Yet, as we seek solutions, we are being asked to curtail our activity within our own parish confines. We will continue to meet somewhere. Our resolve is to persevere, and our voices and numbers will grow stronger until we are heard.

Finally, a priest from Saint Michael's in North Andover wrote a public letter: "A group of dedicated parishioners has formed a chapter of VOTF and have asked to use St. Michael's facilities. Their mission statement says that they want to support the victims of clergy abuse, support priest of integrity and change the church. I have no problem with the first two goals. But I am not clear about the third goal of 'change the church,' nor do I think they are clear as to what this means. What I am sure of, though, is that they are a group of faithful Catholics who are truly concerned about the scandal and cover-up that has shaken the foundation of our church, as I think all Catholics are. They want to provide a place where all people can come together to discuss issues that are troubling them; they want to offer comfort to the victims of abuse and aid in their healing process. Unless they begin to act against the pope and bishops or begin to profess teachings contrary to scripture and tradition, they will be welcomed at St. Michael's."

This letter underscored that there were plenty of priests, despite their own bishop's warnings, who supported VOTF. But, a follow-up letter to the parishioners of St. Michaels from the same priest who welcomed us illustrated that the bishops were in control:

> A month ago, I wrote a letter saying that St. Michael's Church would open its facilities for VOTF meetings unless I received direction from the Cardinal to do otherwise… Yesterday, I received a letter from our Merrimack regional Bishop. He writes: At the present time the Archbishop, Cardinal Law, is in dialog with the leaders of VOTF through his Vicar General, Bishop Edyvean. These conversations aim at the clarification of all the hidden and open issues involved and promoted by VOTF. These issues touch on the essence of our ecclesiology. While these issues remain still unresolved in this dialog, the activities and promotion of VOTF must be curtailed in order to avoid further scandal and polarity among our parishioners… In this great church crisis, I've always tried to remain obedient to the will of the Ordinary. When I was ordained as a priest, I promised always to be obedient to the Archbishop of the Boston Archdiocese and to his successors. Bishop Allue is asking us to discontinue permission to use our parish facilities to VOTF until we await the final judgment. Hopefully in the days ahead, greater integrity, compassionate understanding, and unity can happen throughout our own archdiocese and throughout the church universal. Certainly, some faithful parishioners and non-parishioners alike will continue to meet somewhere else as members of the VOTF. I pray that God's Holy Spirit will bring them great wisdom and I pray that VOTF members will help bring practical and Orthodox solutions and answers to very complicated and challenging issues in our church.

But, every setback was balanced by another letter of support. They came from as far away as Japan, including this e-mail from the Fathers in Kumamoto, Japan:

> Just another message of support for VOTF. I read that bishops and pastors are banning VOTF from dioceses and parishes. It is to be expected because the church automatically reacts to anything new by saying, 'NO!' usually without looking at the facts or situation. I am a missionary working in Japan for the last 40 years. I have found out that the church if it is to have any meaning or value in this world, has to listen and adapt to a variety and diversity of people, places, and cultures. Too long has the church tried to stuff everything into a small box controlled by a small minority who claim to be absolutely right. It just doesn't work. I feel that VOTF is providing a voice for this diversity and freedom. So keep going in the right direction. We need a much bigger church than the one we have now. Peace and Love.

The bans continued, though. We called an emergency meeting to discuss them, and in particular to talk about what to do about the bishop in Rockville, NY, who said that our mission statement is "so vague it leaves the door open for any number of interpretations." It was time to respond. I put out the following:

> VOICE OF THE FAITHFUL CALLS ON BISHOP MURPHY TO RESCIND BAN ON NEW YORK BASED GROUP CHURCH MEETINGS
>
> Voice of the Faithful, a group of over 25,000 lay Catholics formed in response to the ongoing sexual abuse crisis in the Catholic Church, today expresses its deep disappointment to learn that Bishop William F. Murphy has banned VOTF members from assembling on church property in the diocese of Rockville Center, Long Island, NY.
>
> Bishop Murphy states that channels for discussion already exist in Parish Councils and the Pastoral Council. Yet, clergy members lead these councils—not members of the laity who seek their own voice.
>
> In denying Catholics the right to assemble on property built and maintained by their donations, Bishop Murphy inadvertently compounds the pain and outrage felt by parishioners everywhere. We maintain this prohibition is inconsistent with the Spirit of our church

as well as its doctrinal law, and stay committed to continue to organize the lay faithful for our healing and to further the work of the church.

This statement was supported by the Theologian Petition, which we released at the Hynes Center convention. The theologian petition was a shared commitment of the hierarchy, clergy, and laity to address what Pope John Paul II called a story of "Shame and scandal." It required informed and open dialog to discuss the root causes of the problems facing the church. It called for discussion concerning a culture that placed the image ahead of the people, and about a management structure that was not based on the vision of Vatican II.

We were seeking to be an agent of healing and reconciliation, working within the laws of the Catholic Church. We were calling on the bishop to rescind his decision. We stood ready to meet with him to answer questions and provide assurances of our constructive intent. We were ready to assist new chapters on Long Island, across the nation and around the world via organization, self-education regarding the rights and responsibilities of lay Catholics, and by holding prayerful meetings to support the victims and the survivors of clergy sexual abuse.

Notable publications picked up that sentiment, as illustrated in *America*, which concluded that some members of the American Church's hierarchy were fearful of these lay voices, and that they believed these voices would only create confusion and doubt as well as conspire with church enemies to publicize the church's failings. The article went on to point out that folks who joined VOTF were not secularized Catholics who "bashed" the church, and that they took "No pleasure in the church's predicament." I could not have asked for a better overview.

But these bans, as well as issues involving Anthony, and a couple of our speakers at the convention, continued to be major distractions. The key messages were being criticized. A massive, internal debate began to take place within VOTF.

"Every day we are struck by the confusion created by our beloved third goal," said Steve Krueger. "Although many of us view the ambiguity as an invitation for dialog, we all know it will take a long time for us to provide the kind of answers that will satisfy ourselves, let alone our lay critics and, of course, the institutional church. In speaking with some charitable foundations the other day, I was asked why we don't modify goal number three for the sake of clarity. Based on that discussion, I would like to propose an amendment to our third goal. Our third goal was set to shape structural change within the church. I suggest we add, 'based on mutual accountability and shared responsibility, in the spirit of Vatican II.'"

"The word 'shared' bothers me," said a member from our Maine-based group. "It implies that I have something that I believe is mine (but it really belongs to both of us), but I might be willing to share all of it, most of it, some of it, or most likely, a little bit of it with you. I want to participate in the guidance and governance of my church to the fullest extent possible. And Scripture, canon law, and Vatican II gives me permission.

"I think Steve's revision is not an improvement, and I don't support it," Terry said. "We should not add vague language at a time when potential members need us to define ourselves clearly. I strongly agree with Paul, and I would add 'catechism' to his list. Changing the language for our goals would signal a retreat. I believe the word 'change' belongs there.

I believe the word 'shared' is superfluous," said Anthony. "It is sufficient to say, 'based on mutual accountability and responsibility.' From the pope to the last layperson, our accountability is to one another (and the world), within our accountability and responsibility to the Spirit of Christ."

Anthony then pointed out that the phrase "in the spirit of Vatican II" had many difficulties, and he provided some unique insight. "During Vatican II," he said, "the Curia officials said, loudly enough to be heard by us assistants, that when the bishops of the world went home, they (the Curia officials) would take back the church. And for the last 40 years they have worked to do just that, with major help from the present Pope John Paul II, who sees Vatican II as telling the laity that they should be more 'active in the world,' not in the church."

Anthony continued, "The hierarchy is mostly canon lawyers. They focus on what is written—on literal meanings. The expression 'the Spirit of Vatican II' hits them as fuzzy nonsense, reminiscent of the hippies of the '60s. The hierarchy also focuses on power. Many bishops take the expression 'shared' to be a code for 'the laity wanting to take power away from the hierarchy.' In light of all this, I suggest that instead of saying "in the Spirit of Vatican II" we say "in full accord with the teachings of the church."

I didn't care if people had a problem with Anthony. This guy had insights that we needed. He was a trove of information that we couldn't get anywhere else. However, changing the group's messages would indeed signal, not only a retreat, as Terry had pointed out, but would also it would reveal an organization unsure of what it wanted. The goals were left intact.

27. NEW JOB—NEW OFFICE

As the colorful New England leaves began to tumble to the ground, so too did my tech career. Business came to a halt, all software projects and marketing events were canceled, and employees were walking around like zombies. But I didn't care. One hundred percent of my time was now spent on VOTF. If I was at work, I was locked in my office printing off news articles, drafting up releases and running up astronomically high cell phone bills talking to the press.

My manager was laid off in late summer. A new person had been brought in to trim the rolls and get the company ready for sale. I had been praying for a layoff. I didn't have it in me any longer to pitch software. The very idea of spending my time pitching technology seemed a complete waste. *This doesn't help society. The goal is really to increase the company's value, so its executives can receive huge payoffs. How could I have ever made this the center of my world? In the big picture, my financial gain here means nothing!*

I was called into the new manager's office and asked to have a seat in front of his desk. He looked at me, and shuffled some papers. "Thanks for coming in. As you know, this company is going through a lot of changes as we're getting it ready for sale. It's been finalized, the company will be sold to a private equity firm," he said. "I see you've done some good work here, but we're going to have to let you go." He then looked across the desk at me.

I looked back at him, and said, "You and I both know there is nothing left for me to do here and that over the last few months, the entire marketing department has been waiting to be laid off. Just let me know what my severance package is, point me to the paperwork, and I'll be on my way."

The severance package was generous. I was given six months' pay. The timing worked out perfectly. VOTF was now opening up an office in Newton, Massachusetts. Steve Krueger was made interim executive director and given a budget to hire several full-time employees. Steve approached me and said, "I am proud to offer you VOTF's first full-time position, we can't do this without you." This was the greatest validation of my work that I had ever received.

"I know it's only a small fraction of the salary you are used to, but if things continue, we will be able to bump up your pay in the future," Steve added.

"I've been doing this job for about five months now without any pay," I said. "And I will gladly continue to do so, but since I've just been laid off, any money would be greatly appreciated."

Our new office was on the second floor of a small two-story building in Newton. There was a small pond outside, a few thin trees, and a bench. Inside, there was a reception desk with a small waiting area containing a couple of maroon high-back chairs, a coffee table, and a four four-foot tall plant. Around the corner, there was a conference room containing a boardroom-style table, with 12 chairs around it. On the left-hand wall was an enormous whiteboard. The office opened up into its main area, which contained two offices and approximately half a dozen cubicles. Just off to the right was a room that I used to conduct press interviews. I needed a large area to accommodate journalists bringing TV cameras, audio equipment, lights, etc. I hung a large VOTF sign on the wall and always made sure that it was in the background. The opposite end of the room was my work area. There was a six six-foot, white, plastic folding table there, where I would sit with my laptop. To the right of me was a small black-and-white TV with a fire engine red plastic shell. The TV was from the 1970s. I acquired it when I'd bought a brownstone in Chelsea, Massachusetts, and the former owners had left it. That thing served as my tracking system. I always had it on in the background, monitoring local news. At the other end of the table sat a midsize, black, AM/FM, cassette radio. In the same manner as the TV, the radio was always on.

Flanking me on all sides were piles and piles of newspaper articles and magazine clippings. I was now mainly focused on information concerning Cardinal Law. I was looking for anything that would give me a hint as to his next move. *What is he doing? Where is he going? What is he saying?*

There was a ton of news to follow. New allegations of clergy sexual abuse were popping up daily. Journalists turned to us for comment. By fall, what had started as a Boston-based tragedy had spread; newspapers around the country were reporting on it:

Archdiocese of Los Angeles—Cardinal Roger M. Mahony announces the dismissal of 6 to 12 archdiocese priests for accusations of sexual abuse of minors. Mahony refused to divulge their names to the police.

Diocese of Santa Rosa, California—Donald Wren Kimball, a Santa Rosa priest, is convicted by a Sonoma County, California jury for the molestation of a 13-year-old girl in 1981. The same jury acquitted him of raping a 14-year-old girl in 1977.

Archdiocese of Seattle—a priest is placed on leave after being accused by a former altar boy of rape during the 1970s. The priest, who denies the charges, was investigated five years earlier for a similar act. The former altar boy filed a lawsuit against the archdiocese.

Archdiocese of St. Louis—the office of the St. Louis circuit attorney announces that its investigating 50 allegations of sexual abuse by priests after asking victims to come forward. The archdiocese removed three priests, accepted the resignation of a fourth, and placed the fifth on leave.

Diocese of Cleveland—the diocese suspends nine priests pending a review of past sexual abuse allegations. Another priest, Reverend Don A. Rooney, 48, kills himself after an allegation against him dating from 1980 surfaces. In addition, the diocese releases the names of 12 former or retired priests with histories of child molestation. Local prosecutors issue a grand jury subpoena on April 5th requiring the diocese to release all records related to child abuse allegations.

Archdiocese of Cincinnati—Archbishop Daniel E. Pilarczyk announces that about 20 church employees, including some priests, were accused of child abuse in the past. The archbishop has refused to release names.

Diocese of Portland, Maine—district attorneys asked the diocese to release records of sexual abuse accusations dating back 75 years. Attorneys announced that cases for which the statutes of limitation have expired might still yield information leading to new prosecutions.

Diocese of Bridgeport, Connecticut—two priests are removed from their parishes; and a third resigns after admissions of sexual misconduct with minors. The incidents dated from the 1960s and 1970s.

Archdiocese of New York—following accusations that Cardinal Edward Egan had allowed accused priests to stay on the job, the Archdiocese of New York places six priests on leave after allegations of sexual misconduct. The names of the priest were turned over to the district attorney.

Archdiocese of Philadelphia—Cardinal Anthony Bevilacqua calls sexual abuse, "Among the most depraved of moral aberrations," as the archdiocese reveals it had evidence that 35 priests had abused about 50 children over the past several decades.

Diocese of Palm Beach, Florida—Bishop Anthony J. O'Connell resigns following accusations that he molested seminarians.

Not one of these cases would have surfaced if it were not for the brave survivors and the pressure from the court of public opinion brought on by the *Globe's* journalism—and there were thousands upon thousands of more cases on the way.

28. THE GOVERNOR

In October, I worked with Governor Frank Keating's representatives to set up a meeting. The U.S. Catholic Bishops chose him to oversee their efforts to address the clergy sexual abuse problems. Our meeting with him was held at Hanscom Air Force Base. Jim Post attended along with leaders of SNAP. It was a brief conversation. We discussed how to establish a dialog with the bishops, and we asked the governor if he could provide assistance.

I wanted to get him to comment on how our groups were being banned from meeting on church property. After the meeting, the *Globe* wrote the following in an October article: "Keating Questions Banning of Lay Group." "Just because you wear a red hat does not necessarily mean that you have the knowledge of what is going on. You need the input and advice of a wide variety of people," the governor said. "The archbishop here and the bishops elsewhere need to be informed. That means there's got to be far more dialog. We would not be here talking about this if the bishops had handled this properly, but here we are... No one should be afraid of dialog."

I was feeling better now and had renewed energy. That quote helped our groups with their local difficulties. However, the Governor's role did not last long. Dealing with the U.S. bishops proved to be too frustrating for him, and in June of 2003 he resigned. A *Los Angeles Times* interview quoted Governor Keating equating working with the bishops to working with the mafia, "To act like La Cosa Nostra and hide and suppress, I think, is very unhealthy. Eventually, it will all come out."

October was shaping up to be a good press month. Cardinal Law rescinded the ban at St. Michael's in North Andover. This was viewed as a win.

Steve was quoted over the wires, "Although we appreciate Cardinal Law's rescinding of this ban, this situation creates several perplexing questions for us: We don't understand the grandfathering of existing VOTF affiliates, yet the ban of future VOTF affiliates within the same archdiocese, particularly since we as Catholics have every right within church teaching to assemble for the good of our church. Given the fact that there is a continuing misunderstanding of the mission and goals of VOTF on the part of Cardinal Law and the Archdiocese, we don't understand why Cardinal Law hasn't spoken to us directly to hear our answers to his questions.

"To minimize future disruption and pain among our faith family, VOTF calls on Cardinal Law to meet with representatives of VOTF without further delay, and not through intermediaries."

29. AT THE GATES

In mid-October, the world received the Vatican's response to the U.S. Bishops' Dallas Charter for the Protection of Children. In essence, the Vatican vetoed the charter. It found the proposed zero-tolerance policy unacceptable. Instead, the Vatican proposed more time to "reflect" on the issue and created a panel of eight clergymen, four from Rome, and four from the U.S.

The church was refusing to turn over sexual offenders to local authorities. It wanted to handle these matters itself, internally, in secret. Every news outlet covered the story, and I was furious. *After all that's been uncovered! After all that's been documented! After all the lives that have been ruined! What am I missing?* I headed to Watertown, Massachusetts to conduct a live interview with Pat Buchanan on his show, *Buchanan and Press*.

Just before the interview, my cell phone rang. It was *Time Magazine* looking for comments on the Vatican's response to the charter. Their article read:

> VOTF, a lay group that grew out of dismay over the church's handling of the sexual abuse scandal in Boston, called the Vatican's rejection of the Dallas Charter "deeply troubling." Mike Emerton, spokesman for the group, said the response "shows they have no understanding of the depth of this problem." Emerton said that it was unclear why the Vatican required more time to 'reflect' on the charter. "Why they need extra time to reflect on a document they've had for four months is confusing. Rome hasn't gotten the point yet," he said, and he called on the bishops to move immediately to protect children by implementing the Dallas Charter. Since June, a number of bishops have implemented some or all of its policies while others have held off. Since responsibility has once more been given to individual bishops, "There's nothing to stop bishops from implementing the charter provisions immediately." Emerton said, "There's the challenge. The responsibility is once more with the bishops to ensure children are protected, and priests are allowed due process."

I finished the conversation with *Time Magazine* just seconds before going live with Buchanan. The broadcast was a split screen. Buchanan on the left; I was on the right. We went back and forth about homosexual priests, crimes, and the Vatican's lack of response. Buchanan said that the RCC had a responsibility to turn evidence over to the police. He then asked me what the Vatican's response has been. I said the Vatican would not recognize civil authorities. This is one its major problems. I also outlined how it was ridiculous that the bishops needed more time to "reflect" on the Dallas Charter. We then spoke about the new committee the Vatican was forming between U.S. bishops and members of the Curia, to address the situation, statutes of limitation, and the policy to send abusive priests to monasteries for lives of prayer, rather than jail. I ended the conversation by calling for open and honest dialog with the bishops. I wanted the U.S. bishops to rescind their ban on VOTF chapters and join us in a conversation.

After the interview, I was back on the phone with the Associated Press, which reported, "Mike Emerton, criticized this approach as a 'line-item veto,' potentially allowing as many interpretations of the policy as there are dioceses.

Press from all over the world descended upon us. My notebook was running out of pages. As I entered the office, Rose, our volunteer receptionist, handed me a pile of messages as thick as a novel, as well as a plate with a corn muffin on it before returning to the lines on the phone. Every light flashed. I went to my desk, shuffled the messages, and buttered the muffin. Most interesting among the messages was that *Life Magazine* was going to feature us in its "Year In Pictures" edition.

VOTF had scheduled another meeting with Bishop Edyvean. *This time, Donna will not get the best of me. I'll conduct the press my way.* I faxed a news alert to all local media sources and followed up with phone calls. I informed them that VOTF would be available in front of the Cardinal's office immediately after the meeting for comments.

I then loaded a Hewlett-Packard printer and a fresh package of paper into my airport Samsonite with the extendable handle and wheels. One block away from Saint John's Seminary, which was also the Cardinal Law's office and residence, and across from Boston College, was the Espresso Royal Café sitting at the end of the Green Line. Even with the wheels, it was hard to manage the suitcase with a heavy laptop slung over my shoulder, too.

When I arrived at the cafe, I found a table next to an outlet and plugged the printer into the wall. I then unwound the cords, plugged the laptop into the wall, and the printer into the laptop. I pulled out my cell phone, and put it on the table in front of me, and sipped some coffee. Then it rang. The meeting with Bishop Edyvean was over. I put the phone to my ear, and typed, "the meeting was cordial and productive"—but inside, I burned because there was still no progress on the Fund, the bannings, or anything relevant! *What is it about the Catholic Church! Why is it stuck in slow motion? I don't get it!* As I typed, I clenched my teeth and wrote that these issues will be brought up at a face-to-face meeting between Cardinal Law and VOTF at a date to-be-determined. After that, I then proceeded to print 50 copies. Everyone in the cafe turned to stare as the printer grinded. I gathered up the copies, packed-up the printer and asked the young hippie behind the counter if she would store it all for me. "I'm not going to be responsible if it's stolen," she said. I smiled, and with the laptop hanging off my shoulder, I ran the hundred yards back up the street to pass out the release to the press waiting outside Law's gates.

I sprinted toward the Cardinal's office. The press waiting there turned to see me running at them with my mirror sunglasses, pressed suit, and black leather trench coat. They made way. I stood in the middle of them and welcomed them with freshly printed releases. "Get your cameras ready! VOTF members will be exiting those doors and coming up the driveway shortly."

I went into the offices and greeted our delegation in the reception area. I needed to speak with them before we addressed the press. "I adjusted the release, but is there anything else we can say that will show forward momentum?"

"We didn't receive much response on our structural change goal," Bill Cadigan said.

"We told them that VOTF was reenergizing the parishes and that the bannings were causing additional pain and sorrow," Mary Ann added.

Steve said that he requested that a small group of VOTF members meet with Cardinal Law to directly discuss the bannings. As he put it, the bannings were "a subtle form of excommunication."

I then asked the group, "Are you ready to approach the cameras? There is a very large turnout, just outside the main gate."

When I was sure everyone was ready, I threw open the doors, and we began our walk to the gates.

Jim Post approached the microphones with his back against the stone wall that surrounded Saint John's Seminary. Dozens of microphones pointed at him, people stood, crouched, sat, and got up on their toes in the back as the broadcast lights flooded the area. I stood off to the side, ready to clarify or avert.

No more joint releases. This was a preemptive strike. Donna then walked through the doors, up the driveway, and over to the microphones to deliver the Archdiocese's view. Now, she was on the defensive.

30. THE SECOND DREAM

It is black. There is absolutely no light. There is only a voice in my head echoing, resounding, ringing, pulsing, getting bigger and bigger, louder and louder ...

> *Integral to my plan is to confuse all the Marys and slaughter their lambs! Integral to my plan is to confuse all the Marys and slaughter their lambs!*

Again and again! This phrase was being shouted in my head. I tried to cover my ears with my hands, but it was no good. It was coming from everywhere, yet had no source.

> *Integral to my plan is to confuse all the Marys and slaughter their Lambs! Integral to my plan is to confuse all the Marys and slaughter their lambs!*

Louder and louder! I couldn't stop it. And then I was horrified to realize that I was mouthing these words...

> *Integral to my plan is to confuse all the Marys and slaughter their lambs! Integral to my plan is to confuse all the Marys and slaughter their lambs!*

My heart beat faster as the terrible phrase started coming off my tongue!

And then ... it was over.

I was lying on my back, staring at the bedroom ceiling. A cold sweat soaked the pillowcase. My heart began to slow. The pressure was taking its toll. A full night's sleep was impossible. Other members were also experiencing stress. Steve came down with gout and was in extreme pain all the time. Louise was fighting migraines, and everyone in the office had a cold. We were falling apart.

31. THE WORLD TURNS

By November, the public felt that the Vatican was doing nothing to address a scandal that had by then engulfed the globe. Accusations of abuse and cover-up were reported in dozens of countries. The Vatican was trying to mandate a statute of limitations of 10 years after the victim's 18th birthday. If successful, this would insulate the Church from a lot of abuse cases, as it often takes decades for victims to come forward. Bishop Gregory and Cardinal George were defending the Vatican's decision, telling journalists that the Holy See did not weaken what the bishops proposed in Dallas, and that they would put any priest on administrative leave no matter how old the allegation.

What they didn't understand was that there was a breach of trust between the laity and the bishops, as well with society. No one believed that the bishops were going to police themselves or that they would hold themselves responsible.

Cardinal Law began to sound contrite in the press. It seemed as if he was taking some responsibility. At Mass in the Cathedral of the Holy Cross in Boston's South End, he said that he now had a "far deeper awareness of this terrible evil." He went on to say that he had been listening to victims, hearing their stories of how sexual abuse destroyed their lives. "I acknowledge my own responsibility for decisions which led to this intense suffering," he admitted.

I wasn't buying it! I believed that he was taking advice from his PR staff, softening his message to save his ass. The Associated Press contacted me for comment on his recent change of heart, and reported, "Mike Emerton said, 'he still holds Law accountable for his actions over the past two decades, when he moved accused priests from parish to parish. In light of his statement, we must ask ourselves—why did it take him two decades and ten months to come clean in his role in the cover-up?' Emerton also said, 'VOTF is calling on all American bishops to follow Law's example of meeting with victims.'"

On November 10, the U.S. bishops gathered for a conference, this time it was in Washington, D.C. They were there to revise the sexual abuse policy they had created in Dallas. In the same manner as Dallas, we conducted our own press conference before theirs. Ours was at the National Press Club. I drove Susan Troy, Steve Krueger, and Svea Fraser to D.C. in my Montero Sport.

On the way, we all had our laptops open, finalizing messages and speeches. We needed to tighten up what wanted to say. Ideas were shouted back and forth until all the laptop batteries drained. We arrived in D.C. without a consensus, so we worked late into the night.

I had been awake for days trying figure out what the bishops' next move would be and was getting toward the end of a speech that I was writing when my laptop froze.

"Shit!" I screamed.

My roommate, Steve, asked, "What is it?" as he looked over at me from his bed.

"My laptop froze! I didn't save anything yet!"

"Reboot it!" Steve said.

I was too tired, and my frustration level was too high. "Well, it's not coming back on! And I just lost everything! Our entire day's work!" I screamed again as I rapidly pressed the Ctrl+Alt+Delete buttons. Then I grabbed the laptop screen and slammed it shut. A loud cracking sound filled the room. I had a sinking feeling. I slowly opened it back up to see cracked lines spread like a spider web across the screen. The damage was done. I put the laptop on the bed and walked around the room. Steve offered his laptop, and I sat down again to re-create the day's work.

Morning came too early. I only had an hour of sleep. Sucking it up, I hopped in the shower, threw on my suit, and followed Steve to the lobby. There we accompanied Susan and Svea to the conference room. I laid the kits out on a table, went to the podium to check the microphone, and make sure that there was plenty of water.

I noticed that we had fewer journalists than in Dallas. When everyone was settled, with Steve, Susan and Svea at my side, I opened:

> *Good afternoon. October and the first couple weeks in November have proven to be an important time for Voice of the Faithful, and, indeed, Catholics throughout our country. Most recently, U.S. bishops selected the FBI's top ranking woman, Kathleen McChesney, to head the Office for Child and Youth Protection. We pray that her 30-plus years of investigating skills and take charge manner will be permitted to thrive as she ensures that American church leaders adhere to the recent sexual abuse policy. However, we remain skeptical that her employers will enable Kathleen to prosecute offending U.S. bishops.*
>
> *Although we applaud the Bishops for strengthening a fair and due process for accused priests, we question their 'best wisdom' regarding a*

fair and due process for victims of sexual abuse. Clearly, a ticking ten-year clock, counting down the minutes to ignore the deplorable deeds of a sexual offender, is not reflective of the pastoral concern needed for the Catholic Church in the United States.

With regard to the Charter, one important item remains noticeably absent from this revision: accountability for the bishops who created the scandal and worked diligently to cover it up for 30-plus years.

Also accompanying me from Massachusetts is Steve Krueger, Voice of the Faithful's interim executive director. Steve will take a few moments and address the self-defeating edicts by several U.S. bishops to ban Voice of the Faithful from using church property to discuss the Catholic sexual abuse crisis. Currently, bishops in Connecticut, Maine, New York, New Jersey, Oregon, and partially in Massachusetts, have restricted us from using church property while labeling us as "anti-Catholic" and "anti-Church."

Also with us is Svea, joining us this afternoon to urge Catholics to make their views and voices heard by aligning themselves with organizations such as Voice of the Faithful. American Catholics deserve to have a working relationship with the U.S. bishops to address these important issues and help ensure a crisis of this proportion never darkens the doorstep of our churches again. Our faith is too important; we remain steadfast in our determination to provide safe parishes and stand ready to work with the U.S. bishops.

Although, I thought the conference went well, we were missing proof of any change. Discussions were happening, but where were the fruits of all this discussion? I felt the press was looking for something that we couldn't provide, and I grew concerned about VOTF's image of 'relevance' to this crisis.

Notions that I was 'out of my league' assailed me. I keep thinking that VOTF would do much better with a seasoned PR person, someone who had experience dealing with a global crisis. It was at times like these that I would open George Stephanopoulos' book, *All Too Human*, to reread various sections that I had highlighted. One passage in particular gave me comfort: "I wasn't always proud of the way I had handled myself during the campaign. I had learned to calculate, scheme, and maneuver—to say things I didn't fully believe and do things I might later regret while telling myself that, maybe, it would do some good. That night, I had no doubts. I had faith in my candidate, his crowd, and myself. I believed that our compromises and our trials were our contributions to the common good—and that anything was possible if only we could do what had seemed improbable..."

The U.S. bishops were also distributing information to journalists. I approached their table, grabbed a packet, and began to walk away when I heard, "Excuse me. May I see your press pass?"

"I don't have a press pass," I replied.

"Well then, I can't let you have that," the man behind the table said. He held out his hand to retrieve the packet.

I looked at him for a moment, then handed it back. I then bumped into NBC's, Anne Thompson. Anne had been to our offices several times. I asked her if could get one of the bishops' press kits for me.

"You can't just take one?" Anne asked.

"No. They're policing them."

Anne smiled at me, disappeared and then reappeared with a press kit. Digging through the kit, I found exactly what I was after, Bishop Gregory's presidential address. I quickly read it, but I needed a canon lawyer if I was to truly understand it. I soon found one in one Father O. He was a professor of canon law at the Catholic University of America, taught canon law at the Gregorian in Rome, Fordham, and the University of Fribourg. Father O. was the author of nine books and more than two hundred articles on topics in theology and canon law. We had arranged a meeting with him.

He insisted that the meeting be held out in the open, in a public and very noisy place, so we set it up in at a coffee shop in Union Station. Steve, Susan, Svea and I sat down at a table across from Father O. He was at least 80, and his accent was difficult to understand with the din of people shuffling, buzzers going off, and trains arriving and departing. We asked him if the bishops could police themselves, and we needed to know where VOTF stood in the eyes of the Holy See. Father O. focused in on us and from his frail body came a voice of chilling conviction. "You are condemned by association," he said with an icy stare. "We live in a climate of mistrust and fear where both sides are discarded.

My eyes widened as I leaned in toward him.

He extended his finger across the table at us and said, "Disassociation, this is how you get ahead in this climate."

He was referring to VOTF disassociating itself from other groups that Rome had signified as disruptive. Steve then asked what our best method was to make the bishops remove the VOTF bans on church property.

"Hit them in the wallet!" Father O. cried. "This is the only way they will listen to you. Out of a policy of fear and distrust, they will ban you. Bishops see VOTF as breaking up the church. They want unity; VOTF is not under their control. Therefore, you are wrong.

His words pierced me just as much as his stare. He was speaking from decades of experience, and I got the feeling that he'd seen ugly things in the Vatican.

I asked him about the bishops' ability to police themselves, and if they could use the secrecy of confession to withhold information from civil authorities.

"If you take this one away, the secrecy of confession, every bishop will turn against you," he said, sounding a bit like Yoda. "Once you open up this door, you can never close it. It's not the business of the priest to turn a confession into a conversation."

"What about the laity, and our involvement in helping the church?" Steve asked.

"Bishops see the church as perfect. Thus no healing is necessary," Father O. informed us.

Then, Father O. leaned deep into the middle of the table and pointed his finger right at me, "Be careful. You have no idea about the people you are dealing with, and to what extents they will go to protect what is theirs."

The words caused chills. This man was no joke. I swallowed hard, stopped taking notes, and just stared at him.

32. THE CARDINAL

On November 26, we were finally granted a meeting with Cardinal Law. As I traveled down Commonwealth Avenue heading toward his office, I listened to my interview on WBUR. "VOTF is going into this meeting in an open and honest dialog," I heard myself say, "and we expect an open and honest dialog in return."

I parked the car and found Mary Scanlon, Jim Post, Bill Cadigan, and Steve Kruger sipping coffees on the sidewalk. I joined them. We talked about the morning news, and I pressed the question, "How can Cardinal Law keep making bad decisions? Our group could be the Archdiocese's best friend in terms of PR if they would work with us."

"I am fully prepared to come out of this meeting and say it was a complete failure if need be," Jim Post replied.

I gazed across the street toward Saint John's Seminary, toward Cardinal Law's office--with all its eminence and opulence--and I noticed that news trucks were gathering outside along the stone wall. I had faxed a media alert and called all local journalists who were now heading toward the Chancery. I headed in the opposite direction, one block away, to the Espresso Royal Café. I had my printer in my Samsonite again, and my laptop over my shoulder. I found my table by the outlet, went to the counter, and ordered a yogurt with fruit on the bottom.

After two hours of waiting, Jim called. "At last!" I said loudly into the cell phone. The café's patrons turned my way. "What can I put in the release?"

Jim gave me a brief description of absolutely nothing: The bannings were still in place. There was no decision to accept any funds raised by VOTF, and we were told to direct to any questions that we might have to the Archdiocese's Office of Healing and Assistance Ministry. I feared the press would now see the group as useless and unable to affect change.

There wasn't much I could do. I added statements, printed copies, told the person behind the counter to keep an eye on my printer, and then ran up the sidewalk toward the press waiting outside the stone wall of Cardinal Law's administrative offices.

The air was cold. It settled into my chest. I ran as fast as I could. Protesters had gathered on the sidewalk blocking my way, so I jumped up onto the stone wall and ran past them toward the cameras and journalists. I jumped off the wall and landed close to a reporter from The *New York Times*.

"Hi Katie," I said in a labored breath.

Taking a moment to recover from her shock, she said, "Quite an entrance. Are you ready?"

"I need about ten more minutes with our delegation."

Then I turned around to the large group of reporters and screamed, "Ten more minutes!"

I ran through the gates and toward the office where the group was meeting. When I entered the building's lobby, I was surprised to see that no one from VOTF was waiting for me, so I grabbed a seat and waited for them. A few minutes later, the doors to the meeting room opened, and to my surprise it was not one of our members coming through them, but was instead Cardinal Law. He stepped into the lobby and noticed me. He extended his hand, and, with a smile, asked, "What is your name?

Taking his hand firmly, I looked right into his eyes and said, "Mike Emerton, I'm the spokesperson for Voice of the Faithful." The smile instantly faded from his face, he withdrew his hand and walked out the door.

The delegation came out about 30 seconds after he left. I gathered them around to see if there was anything else that we wanted to say to the press, but there was nothing. I opened the door and signaled to the press waiting outside that we were about to come out. Taking the signal, cameramen focused their lenses on the doors and followed us as we walked outside the gates to the podium set up on the sidewalk.

Jim took the microphone.

Voice of the Faithful today held its first face face-to to-face meeting with Cardinal Bernard Law. Although the dialog was cordial, no decisions were made regarding the Voice of Compassion Fund, or the lifting of bans on our group from meeting on church property.

Our discussion was a frank and candid exchange of views. We have taken the first step. Cardinal Law noted our good work with survivors of clergy sexual abuse and agreed that we should work together to achieve just results.

We are disappointed that Cardinal Law has made no decision regarding the $56,000 in heartfelt donations given by over 250 faithful Catholics

> to the Voice of Compassion Fund. Cardinal Law did inform the group that he needed additional materials. It was agreed that a meeting will be held between VOTF and the Chancellor of the Archdiocese, in order to continue the dialog on the Voice of Compassion Fund.
>
> Cardinal Law has not yet decided to rescind the ban on VOTF groups from meeting on church property, a ban that affects approximately 320 parishes throughout the Boston Archdiocese. This retention of bannings guarantees continued pain for thousands of faithful Catholics who wish to use their church facilities for discussions. VOTF continues to believe that it is immoral and self-defeating for bishops to ban parishioners from using buildings that they have paid for and continue to support through financial donations. VOTF will continue to challenge such bans.
>
> With regard to the Charter for the Protection of Children and Young People, Cardinal Law agreed that collaboration between members of Voice of the Faithful and the Archdiocese's Office of Healing and Assistance Ministry is appropriate and desirable.

Then Donna spoke:

> The purpose of the meeting this morning, from the perspective of Cardinal Law, was to obtain greater clarity on how Voice of the Faithful, as an organization, sees itself in relationship to the church and how it would hope to be seen and recognized by the church. Within this Archdiocese, the Archdiocesan Pastoral Council, and within parishes, the parish pastoral councils are the normal channels for ongoing pastoral planning involving the lay faithful. The Archdiocesan Finance Council and parish finance councils have specific responsibilities delineated in canon law. While the emergence of new groups is a constant in the history of the church, a proper discernment must always take place to ensure their compatibility with the faith, discipline and mission of the church. Today's meeting was a step in that discernment concerning the Voice of the Faithful on the part of the Archbishop.

I was growing frustrated with our message. Time was running out. It seemed to me that we were starting to fade into obscurity. The following day, I received a synopsis of the meeting. Jim informed me that the meeting started out badly: "We had just sat down at the table when Cardinal Law stood up. He pointed his finger right in our faces and said, 'You have done nothing and have had no effect!' He then let the group know that he had everything under control and that he had been meeting with survivors and priests. We all just looked at each other. Then, he shot down every one of our proposals. When Steve said that we had sent a letter to the bishops, he screamed, 'Who are you to be sending letters to the bishops without informing me first?!'"

The words of Father O. warning me to beware of who I was dealing with came back and echoed in my head.

33. THE PHIL DONAHUE SHOW

A day after the meeting with Law, the *Phil Donahue Show* called to say that they wanted to do a show with VOTF. They asked me to help fill the audience. The panel was to be composed of Bill Donohue, President of the Catholic League; David Clohessy, Executive Director of SNAP; Carmen Durso, an attorney representing victims of abuse in the Boston area; Steve Kruger, VOTF's Executive Director; and Boston editor/publisher Chuck Colbert of the *National Catholic Reporter*, who was interviewed via remote video.

To fill the audience, I contacted every VOTF member in New York City and New Jersey and invited them to the show. We had a huge turnout, and I left the green room to welcome them. Standing in the audience, I reached into my pocket and pulled out a stack of 3x5 index cards with questions. I suggested if they were called upon that they introduce themselves as members of VOTF, name what parish they were from, and then ask the question on the card. They all agreed.

I then went back to the green room to speak with Steve and let him know that Bill Donohue was going to be the panel's antagonist. We did not know this until the last minute… something the producer had carefully kept secret. I had a Palm7 (a predecessor to today's smartphones), and to get the most recent information on Bill Donohue, I had to go out to the sidewalk to get reception.

And then it was show time!

The first half of the show involved arguments concerning church finances and whether or not homosexuals should be allowed in the priesthood. During the first commercial break, the producer informed the audience that the next segment was their opportunity to ask questions.

When the show came back, Phil said that the days of "Pay, Pray and Obey" were gone. He emphasized that members of SNAP and VOTF are the ones that who want to remain involved in the Catholic Church, but would like to see the church address its problems in an open and forthright manner. Phil then went into the audience with the microphone and one after another VOTF members stood up and introduced themselves as members from various local parishes and asked their prepared questions. VOTF quickly became the primary presence on the show.

At the next commercial break, I went to speak with several members in the audience. I created new questions. The show's producer waved her arms, motioning for me to talk to her. She was furious, "What the hell are you doing? This is not a Voice of the Faithful show!" she screamed at me.

"Why, whatever do you mean?" I retorted.

"Every person that stands up introduces themselves as a member of Voice of the Faithful. I want that to stop now!"

"Let me get this straight. First you ask me to fill this place with our members, and now you want me to tell them they can't ask any questions? Am I getting that right?"

"This is not a Voice of the Faithful show! I want it to stop!"

"Okay, how about this. I will go into the audience and tell them that The Phil Donahue Show's producer has a problem with them being members of Voice of the Faithful. And I then will ask them to get up and leave. I would say that by looking at this audience, half of it would disappear. Those empty seats are going to look really funny when Phil comes back. Is that what you want?"

I knew we had only a few more seconds before the break was over, and she knew it as well. She stared at me for a moment and then stomped away. I returned to my seat in the front row.

The show was a hit. In an e-mail to VOTF's leadership, Anthony wrote, "Congratulations to all the VOTF people for a wonderful show. VOTF came through as an adult, deeply concerned, positive solution to the church's present tragedy. This showed through, especially in contrast to Bill Donohue's hysterical ignorance. Steve, your input was terrific! We loved your statements that VOTF is a part of the solution, and that the days of hierarchical power are over."

34. BREAKING THE RING

At the beginning of December, the Boston Archdiocese complied with a court order to turn over 11,000 pages of records to plaintiff's attorneys. Judge Sweeney noted that, contrary to Cardinal Law's testimony, these new records showed that priests who had molested children were given new parish assignments even though church officials had reason to believe they were continuing to abuse children.

During the November meeting with VOTF, Cardinal Law had boasted about his record of protecting children from sexual abuse. He said several times that he was personally committed to creating the most effective protection policy in the nation and that he was determined to clean up all old cases involving sexual abuse.

These new documents pointed to a pervasive pattern of administrative cover-up by Cardinal Law, his auxiliary bishops, and others in the hierarchy of the Catholic Church. In addition to this, a church finance council was authorized by Cardinal Law to seek bankruptcy protection for the Boston Archdiocese, which faced an estimated 450 claims from victims. Cardinal Law was losing his base. The wealthiest and most powerful Catholics in Boston publicly registered their anger about this latest revelation in the *Globe*.

Advertising executive Jack Connors Jr., one of the most influential Catholics in Boston, called for Law to go. "The Cardinal has admitted he made mistakes. There is no question that he has made many," said Connors. "It would be an additional mistake for him to attempt to lead after all these disclosures." Noting that contributions to parishes were down by as much as 40 percent, Connors said. "We need to get Cardinal Law to resign, so we can get back to our mission, which is helping the poor."

Public relations specialist Thomas P. O'Neill III, the former lieutenant governor and adviser to Law, also said that a bankruptcy filing would underscore moral shortcomings in the archdiocesan leadership. "What's really too bad is we have the head of the archdiocese and the head of the American church talking about a financial bankruptcy that is very closely associated with moral bankruptcy."

On Sunday, December 8, Cardinal Law did not show up to say Mass at The Cathedral of the Holy Cross. He was in Rome asking the pope to accept his resignation. Instead of the Cardinal, two to three hundred protesters had shown up to demonstrate their disgust at the recent news. It was another chilling December morning as I drove to the protest. Even with the windows up, I could hear the noise a block away. *This can't all be coming from the people at the Cathedral?* I looked up and noticed a bumper sticker on the car in front of me. It read: "Law Must Go!"

When I got there, it was clear to me that this was the largest protest yet. I shook hands with some reporters and members from victim advocate groups. A microphone and podium were set up. Individuals took turns shouting their anger at Cardinal Law. This was a new level! A smoking gun had been found in Law's hands.

I climbed to the top of the Cathedral's front steps to get a better view. I turned around. The sun was shining on me. I opened my leather coat to let the sun hit me in the chest and stood there taking it all in. *This is it! Cardinal Law will never recover from this.* I looked across the crowd and thought about Father Paquin, and how he was a known sexual predator, yet was sent to my hometown. Then I thought about Jimmy Francis's funeral, and what a disgrace, what an abomination, what a violation of everything sacred it was for Paquin to preside over it, and then embrace Jim's grieving friends and relatives like he, too, was a victim. I thought about how I felt after that funeral, how I wanted to burn down St. John the Baptist and wipe it off the earth.

But I also thought about my relationship with God, and how I was being pushed into my work with VOTF, and about Janis, who was now pregnant with our first child. And I thought about how I yearned for simpler times and how I just wanted this all to be over.

I then noticed my breath coming out in large billows, and I played with it. Taking it in and blowing it out like a dragon on top of the steps. I then turned and faced the mammoth doors leading into the church. I tugged them. They creaked opened. There were only a handful of people in the pews. The priest was saying Mass. I knelt down in the back and began to pray. I asked God to please guide us and make sure that we were all doing the right thing—not only in the best interest of Catholics but for everybody. I then dropped my forehead onto my folded hands, and I asked God to release me. I said that I was tired of the pain and hurt and that I was hoping he felt my work was done.

Outside, the protesters had formed a human chain, encircling the cathedral. They held hands and began singing. Their song penetrated the walls. A soft, beautiful wave of harmony came in—it pulsed against my neck and washed against my back, putting my mind and body at ease, and my heart blissfully to rest.

35. LAW MUST GO!

Early in December, 58 Boston-area priests signed a three-page letter calling for Cardinal Law's resignation. They took no pleasure in this and dreaded the Vatican's response.

Excerpts of the letter read as follows:

Dear Cardinal Law:

It is with a heavy heart that we write to request your resignation as Archbishop of Boston. We have valued the good work you have done here in Boston, including, but not limited to: your advocacy for the homeless, your outreach to the Jewish community, your opposition to capital punishment, and your leadership in welcoming immigrant peoples. However, the events of recent months and, in particular, of these last few days, make it clear to us that your position as our bishop is so compromised that it is no longer possible for you to exercise the spiritual leadership required for the Church of Boston.

As leaders of many parishes that make up this Archdiocese, we hear from the people their call for a change in leadership. The revelations that have come to light a few days ago challenge the credibility of your public statements. The people of this archdiocese are angry, hurt, and in need of authentic spiritual leadership. We believe that despite your good work in the past you are no longer able to provide that leadership.

While this is obviously a difficult request, we believe in our hearts that this is a necessary step that must be taken if healing is to come to the archdiocese. The priests and people of Boston have lost confidence in you as their spiritual leader.

The three-page letter was hand-delivered to Law's Brighton residence, but the Cardinal wasn't home. He had vanished. Not even his closest associates could confirm where he was, or if he would keep his appointments. Shortly after the 11,000 pages of damaging information was released, Cardinal Law had secretly flown to Rome and was asking the pope to protect him.

Realizing his cowardice, 100 VOTF members gathered on a cold Wednesday evening in the basement of Our Lady Help of Christians Church in Newton, Massachusetts, to vote on whether the group should officially call for Cardinal

Law's resignation. Over the course of the last ten months, I had attended many meetings here, but this one was different. The room had a new level of anger, a different kind of tension and sorrow. The most prevailing sensation was utter betrayal. Rows and rows of folding chairs were filled with mothers, fathers, grandmothers, lawyers, plumbers, accountants, chefs, businessmen, CEOs, housewives, doctors, retirees, everyone was there in those chairs that evening. I stood in the back, as usual, with my back against the wall, surveying the crowd.

Jim Post opened the meeting, "By nearly any standards, revelations made in early December mark a major turning point in what has been a year of startling disclosures. The facts revealed in these documents point to a pervasive pattern of complicity and cover cover-up by Cardinal Law, his auxiliary bishops, and others in the hierarchy of the Catholic Church."

His eyes narrowed, and his voice took on a tone of conviction, "The crisis of spiritual and moral leadership that has affected the Archdiocese of Boston for nearly one year has accelerated in dangerous and unprecedented ways. Whatever thoughts we had of serious discussion with Cardinal Law about the relationship between himself, as bishop, and Voice of the Faithful, have ended. As I have publicly stated in recent days, the Archdiocese of Boston has effectively been without a bishop. There has been no pastoral presence. The magnitude of this crisis is breathtaking. This crisis is not only a local matter for the 2 two million Catholics in the Archdiocese of Boston, but also a matter for more than 60 million Catholics throughout the United States. We are directly affected. The disclosures point to administrative practices involving other dioceses and, perhaps, the Vatican itself. The systematic gap and extent of this concealment affect every bishop in every diocese of the United States. Individually, and collectively, they are all under suspicion."

It was tense as Jim Post called for each individual to vote. The majority, 71, had called for Cardinal Law's resignation.

On Thursday, December 12, the *Boston Globe* reported that Cardinal Law received a subpoena to appear before a state grand jury looking into criminal violations by church officials who supervised priests accused of sexually abusing children. Along with Law, additional subpoenas were issued for Bishop Thomas V. Daily of Brooklyn, New York, Bishop John B. McCormack of Manchester, New Hampshire, Archbishop Alfred C. Hughes of New Orleans, Louisiana, Bishop Robert J. Banks of Green Bay, Wisconsin and Bishop William F. Murphy of Rockville Centre, New York, many of them whom had been banning VOTF from meeting on church property.

By Friday, it was becoming clear that the pope would accept Law's resignation. The information was confirmed by several of VOTF's Vatican sources, as well as close members of the press. I knew this was the most important press conference VOTF would ever conduct. Friday night, I gathered members of the group at the Newton office to work through our statements. As I left my house at 5 AM the following morning to head back to the office, I gazed up at the stars, which were still shining brightly. I looked for my special star. "Please, guide me through this day and soon all this craziness will be over.

As I headed south on 95, Susan Troy called me. "I just heard from my contact in Rome that the pope accepted Law's resignation," she said in a sobering voice.

"Do the others know?" I asked.

"I'm making some calls, now," she said.

"Good! Let's have everyone meet at the office as soon as possible."

When I arrived, the phones were ringing. I gathered everyone. We finalized our statement and decided to deliver it in front of the office. I issued a media alert and started hitting the phones. About half an hour later, broadcast trucks began pouring into the parking lot. When we reached maximum audience capacity, I called everybody back into Steve's office for one last talk.

"You folks ready for this?" I said to the group as my eyes gazed from one face to the other. "History is on your doorstep."

Then I led a delegation down our steps and out into the parking lot. We stood in a single long line with Jim Post at the center, and Jim delivered the following:

The Archdiocese of Boston has endured a year of terrible suffering brought on by the clergy sexual abuse crisis. Today's announcement of a change in the leadership of the archdiocese is a sad, but a necessary, step in the healing process.

This is not a joyous time for us. Our hearts are heavy with sadness for the damage that has been done to the office of the Archbishop of Boston. We need to emphasize that Cardinal Law's resignation is only a first step. It is not the conclusion to this crisis, nor is it the ultimate solution. Solutions need the "sunlight" of truth and reconciliation in order to bring about healing. Solutions must involve collaboration among the

> *laity, priests, religious, and hierarchy and we urge Bishop Lennon to hear us and act in a spirit of collaboration and collegiality with the laity, survivors and clergy of the Archdiocese of Boston.*
>
> *The archdiocese faces an enormous challenge. Healing requires listening to one another, to survivors and their families, to priests, the religious, and to the laity, women and men of goodwill who share responsibility for the well-being of the church. We must listen to one another, and we must have a real and honest dialog. We must cooperate in shaping solutions. We need a blueprint to heal the Catholic Church. Voice of the Faithful stands ready to begin that work today.*

It was a proud moment for me, but the work had just begun. We now had hundreds of press requests to fulfill, so I turned the office into a command center, creating a dynamic schedule on the office's whiteboard, and matching the best best-fitting spokespersons to each interview request, times, and place. Like the trading floor on Wall Street, I shouted names and filled orders:

> ...Stephanie at ABC's Good Morning America wants someone on camera in Needham to talk about where the movements stand today. Steve, can you take that?... Adam from New England Cable News needs and update. Svea, can you do that after taping the Emily Rooney Show?... Pam from the Washington Post called again. Steve, can you take that on the way to ABC?... Bill from the Chicago Tribune is at the Marriott in Boston and wants to meet a VOTF member. Who do we have downtown?... CJ from the New York Times wants a photo of James Muller. Mary Ann, can you see where he is at?... Diana from the Today Show wants someone to fly out tonight. Who do we have left?... Lester at MSNBC and Betty at the CBS Evening News are looking for comment. Jim, can you take that?... Jessica at Fox is looking for someone to go to Watertown for the Geraldo Rivera show... CNN is looking for someone to be on a debate panel... Lori from CNBC wants a live interview at 4:30. Jim, can you do it?...

And so it went throughout the day until I collapsed on my desk in front of my little red, plastic TV. On the way home, it was late and dark. I looked back up at my star, and thinking of Janis, I said in my heart, "It's finally over, I'm coming home!"

36. THE OPERA HOUSE

My black leather trench coat flowed over the white marble steps as I ascended under the chandelier. Giant stone columns held an ornate ceiling. Highly polished marble floors, pillars and walls gleamed, mirrors radiantly beamed, and angels flew in frescos. Everything was glossy, and it seemed that people were pointing at me, whispering, as I passed by. It seemed like they were pointing and saying, "That's him. That's one of the people that kicked the cardinal out of Boston. That's him. I recognize his coat. He's the one that spoke from the pews, a voice of the people."

Well, maybe not that, but something like that, because it did seem that people on this grand night in Boston were recognizing me—recognizing me as the man who overcame his abuse, who reversed his course, who rose above his affliction, and then who went on a hero's quest to restore the church. Well, maybe not that. But judging by the ratings numbers, certainly a lot of people had been watching, and some probably recognized me, as I walked those steps with Janis. Some surely had been paying attention as I tried over the last year to get Cardinal Law to be upfront and honest, to deal with the scandal, to reach out and heal the victims, help them become survivors… but instead of that happening, they all watched in horror as the church insulated itself, blamed the victims and hid.

Janis and I took our seats in the Wang Center and waited for the "The Nutcracker" to begin. I hadn't been there since that night with those infernal feet, not since Flatley and his fiendish tights. So much had passed since then, so much had been released, so much had come rushing forth, and so much had crumbled. I sat back in my seat, and this time, instead of those feet, I heard tinkling chimes and soothing violins. And when I opened my eyes, I saw wooden toys dancing, a ballerina spinning, and from the depths of the stage an enormous Christmas tree rising, twinkling as it did every year to a height unimaginable. The tree was up! The dancers dancing, the cymbals crashing, and the gifts piled high. I gently took Janis's hand and kissed it. Then, I looked into her eyes.

*****

Two years later, we were unwrapping Christmas tree ornaments in the living room. Boxes taken down from the attic were stacked everywhere. The newspaper-wrapped stars, shepherds, elves, and snowmen were, once again freed. Janis and I were discussing the tree's symmetry when we noticed that our 1st first-born son, Aidan, had crawled over the rug to a pile of crumpled up newspapers and made a bonnet out of an old page. We laughed. Then we stopped laughing and looked at each other, the paper was the front page of the *Boston Globe* with a big picture of Cardinal Law on the day he stepped down. Janis took the old page off our son's head, crumpled it up and threw it on the floor, but I picked it up, opened it up and looked at those flabby jowls. That whole year came back, and I remembered the pain and the pressure and the fear and the courage it took. *What a year! And now here is my son! But what religion is he going to follow if any? And what will I tell him about the meaning of Christmas? What am I going to say about why those shepherds are standing around that crib, or why the wise men are bringing gifts? What am I going to tell him about all this? What star is he going to follow?*

Well, I didn't know... as I held the crumpled Cardinal in my hands. I didn't know what religion my child would follow. Gentle, peaceful Buddhas went by in my mind... and then an elephant god with many arms, Rabbis with curly sideburns came to my mind, and then those statues on Easter Island looked off into the distance... and I had no idea what set of beliefs I would pass on to my son. I started to get a little worried about that; but, then again, I took some kind of comfort that maybe things were different for Aidan. Maybe we had evolved in some way. Maybe he would be able to go out on his own adventure, to find his own guiding light in the darkness, and there was something about that I liked. There was something about not being tied to dogma and subjected to unquestionable authority that would allow my son to be far freer than I was, and yet there was also a sadness to that in me as I looked at the shepherds haphazardly placed on the mantel, seeming like they were wandering in different directions, and I looked at the animals, which seemed to be straying, leaving Mary and Joseph kneeling alone in the crèche, staring into an empty crib.

CODA

Father Ronald H. Paquin pleaded guilty in December 2002 to three counts of child rape and was sentenced to 12–15 years in prison. In October of 2015, Paquin, who psychologists say admitted to molesting at least 14 boys, was released from state custody after two medical specialists determined he did not meet the legal criteria for sexual dangerousness.

In December 2002, Cardinal Law fled the United States for Rome to evade prosecution. In May of 2004, Pope John Paul II appointed Law Archpriest in charge of the Basilica di Santa Maria Maggiore. Law continued the prestigious position of archpriest until November 21, 2011, when he was replaced.

Voice of the Faithful continues its quest to ensure the Catholic Church is free from child molesters while seeking meaningful, administrative change within a transparent and honest environment. Active groups can be found in many countries.

In 2003, Mike left Voice of the Faithful and returned to the high-tech marketplace. He still resides in Massachusetts and opened BridgeView Marketing, a public relations practice focusing on technology, located in Portsmouth, NH, in 2006. In 2015, Mike and Janis divorced but retain joint custody of their two boys. Mike also began the process of pursuing a case against Paquin.

ABOUT THE AUTHORS

Michael Emerton grew up in Haverhill, MA, earned an Associate Degree in Aviation from North Shore and a Bachelors Degree is Business at Salem State College. Michael is a respected PR expert with extensive technology experience in enterprise management software, LAN/WAN architectures, wireless communications and crisis management experience for corporate and not-for-profit organizations. His PR initiatives first have garnered national attention as he worked with 3Com and The Commission on Presidential Debates, to provide 1000 press members in the 2000 Presidential Debates with their first broadband connectivity for filing stories and photos via 3Com's Visitor Base Networks. Notable are Michael's crisis management skills, where he developed and delivered key messages to the press for Voice of the Faithful, a lay Catholic organization seeking changes within the church. His PR guidance brought global fame to the group.

Patrick Emerton grew up in Haverhill, MA; earned English and Film Studies degrees from Boston College; was a cast member in the improv troupe My Mother's Fleabag, and co-founder of Every Mother's Nightmare; a Jesuit donné of the Wisconsin Province; member of Annex Theater in Seattle; oyster shucker at the Union Oyster House in Boston; school bus driver for Red Cloud School in Pine Ridge; and an elder care provider. Currently, advocating for special needs, teaching, film consulting, writing, and taking pictures in New England.

www.ingramcontent.com/pod-product-compliance
Lightning Source LLC
Chambersburg PA
CBHW071513040426
42444CB00008B/1620